Savvy Stock Investing

Written by:

Louis Rubin

Researched by the Staff of:

Wealth Achievers, Inc.

List of Advisories

Advisory 1

The Investor

1. *The human factor in investing.* –Investments turn out well or ill according to the progress or retrogression on the company whose bonds or stocks are bought. Investments prove profitable or sources of loss, often, not because of internal factors but because of the cyclical swings of the stock and bond markets. These are the materials and the fields of investment and they form properly the chief subjects of investment analysis. But a third factor is the investor themselves. He is probably as important as either of the others and he may be the most important of the three, for it is upon his interpretation, decision and action that advantage is taken of the movements of the market or that movements are missed; it is his analysis or lack of it which is the determining element in the choice of the securities which comprise the Investment list.

There is no way of measuring the matter statistically but a realistic approach to the investment problem must recognize that money is made or lost probably as often through matters which are primarily psychological as through the success or failure of the companies and the tidal swings of the securities markets. There is not the occasion or the space for a lengthy exposition of the peculiarities of investment psychology, but a treatment of the subject of investments would be incomplete without touching upon some mental traits which are so general as to be characteristic of a great majority of the investment making public. Knowledge of securities and of the markets must be supplemented by that admonition given centuries before there were securities markets: "Know thyself."

2. *The long-range view.* – In the discussions of security analysis emphasis has been laid upon the unimportance of the results of a single year or two. By attention to this factor, the investor will avoid one of the most undesirable of habits, that of being swayed always by the crowd. If the period is one of prosperity, the fact that a company normally earning $3 per share is now earning $7 or $8 will attract heavy buying. It ought not to attract an investor with the long-range view.   It is possible that a new stage of growth is being reached" but it is probable that the exceptional earnings will be as ephemeral as the emotional stage of the bull market and that with the passing of the prosperity phase of the cycle, the earning power will revert to normal. The long-range view should look upon exceptionally large earnings as indicative of a opportune time for selling and subnormal earnings as providing the opportunity for buying.

    Another tangible value of the long-range view is that an investor who adheres to it must recognize the temporary state of any given condition of the market. Until some state of balance in economic affairs is achieved, which will be in truth a new era, the one absolutely certain thing about prices is that they will change and that changes may be both upward and downward. There has never been, and there cannot well be, in the present composition of economic society, anything like a dead level, either of prosperity or depression.

    It is a normal thing that in times of prosperity spirits are ebullient and hopes are high. Then is the time for the investor to take account of the inevitable impending change and to prepare for it. It is equally normal that, when unemployment is rife, factories are partially shut down, and dividends are being omitted on all sides, the spirits of the brokerage fraternity and of investors and speculators run low. Then is the time for the investor with the long-range view to put to practical use his sure knowledge that no depression is endless – and that every depression undoubtedly will be short of a condition which would mean a veritable upheaval of the social structure.

3. *Acting against the crowd.* –It necessarily follows that at times of bubbling optimism and at times of black pessimism the investor will act contrary to the crowd. He will do so on no smug reflection that "the crowd is always wrong." It is not always wrong. He will do so because he knows that a the investment market is partly emotional and, at the two extremes of optimism and pessimism, acting contrary to the crowd is correct and profitable because bull market always follows bear market, and panic - major or minor- is the almost invariable successor of a bull market.

4. *Acting with the crowd.* –But if it is the part of judgment to act contrary to mass action at extremes of bull and bear marke3ts, it does not follow that the same policy is desirable at

4

other times. Acting against the crowd while a bull or a bear market is in progress is probably one of the most costly and futile policies known in the market. When a bull market is in full swing and when it has run only for a short time, to sell is , for an investor, to take the chance which will almost certainly fun against him. The chance taken is the securities parted with can be picked up lower –but the very trend of the market makes the odds run strongly against this as a probability. For a speculator to buck a bull market trend by selling short is one of the most effective roads to financial suicide. The effects are rapid and often so effective as to leave little hope of recovery. The reverse of this process is equally undesirable either for investor or speculator. When the price trend has turned definitely downward there is the tendency to indulge in the expensive pastime of feeling for the bottom. A stock which sold at 100 a few months previously may appear cheap by comparison at 80. But if the trend of the general market is still downward there is not the slightest assurance that it will not reach 60 or 40 or any other lower figure, from which by comparison, a price of 80 would appear extremely high.

In summary of the policy of acting either with or against the crowd, the principle is suggested of traveling on the side on which there is the most company but not to linger in the matter of leave- taking once the destination is reached.

5. *Courage.* –In few fields of economic activity is courage so much a requisite as in the handling of funds. When conditions are all favorable and nearly any security of the worth shows rapid and ample appreciation in short term, the securities market is a place for the brave and the timorous alike. As a matter of fact they cannot be distinguished. But when conditions, on the surface, are most adverse; when the papers are full of discouraging business news; when the market sink in sickening succession of falls which seem endless, the caliber of an investor is put to the test. If, to the long-range view, courage is added, an investor may emulate that Rothschild who –buying consols at a low figure –in answer to an interrogatory as to how he could act with such certainty, replied that if the future were certain consols would not be selling at any such figure. More than this, the right amount of iron in the investor's constitution will keep him from that fairly frequent and disastrous action of the timid –selling out at the bottom. If, in every bear market, an accurate census could be taken, the numbers of the faint hearted who loss courage when prices are almost at the turning point would be valuable illustration of the importance of the single human quality –nerve- on the financial fortunes of the investment fraternity. The boy who shakes his fist at that adversary on the other side of a fence but who runs when both are on the same side is unlikely to be a great fighter, whatever other success he may achieve. The investor who is brave when prices are high and afraid to move when they are low, or who moves only to run away, has a psychological hurdle to overcome.

6. *Stubbornness.* –But not all courage is wisely used. One of the most prevalent and money0losing traits of investors is a blind stubbornness –a determination to adhere to a program, or to retain securities, or to dispose of securities, despite the fact that evidence

pointing to the desirability of an opposite policy may be clear enough for the main in the street to read . The most costly manifestation of this trait is clinging to an investment, or to a line of investments, in a market which is plainly and decidedly headed lower. Now, if a decline, however severe appears to be but a passing phase, there may be reason for not disturbing the bulk or a good sized portion of an investment list, although in a falling market a good-sized reserve of cash or cash equivalent is desirable. But there is no warrant for retaining an entire list in the face of a bear market, or for retaining an entire a single investment if developments indicate that it is less desirable than had appeared to be the case when it was bought. Yet instances abound of positions taken in securities at what turns out to have been an inflated price, and maintained for years.

An investor must know himself well enough to discern when his adherence to a policy is bravery and when it is bravado. One of the oldest axioms of Wall Street is that it never pays to argue with the market, and, as it applies to the investor, this means that when the market says "sell" it is best to heed it even though the market's decision may be contrary to the investor's own judgment, or the reasons for the behavior of the market may not be apparent. In this respect investors, as a body, would do well to take a leaf from the book of speculators. A trader, operating for rapid turnover and small profits, is alert in cutting his losses short. An investor ought to be no less alert. Because he expects larger gains than the speculator he can afford to take larger losses, but if an investor is cashing in average profits of, say, 20 to 25 per cent in favorable markets, he cannot afford to let his holdings depreciate to points where his losses eat up 5 or 10 per cent.

A system for handling investments should be worked out so that losses are taken quickly enough on declines to conserve at least 60 per cent of realized profits. For example, if $5000 has been made through acceptance of profits on a rising market, it is time to be on the alert to sell remaining securities at the first evidence of a turn in the trend so that no more than $2,000 will be lost.

7. *Bargains and pseudo-bargains.* –The market reflects extremes of pessimism and of optimism, and it is frequently wrong in overdoing expectations when business is rising, or in discounting too much when business is declining. But in the long run the market is right. An investor must remember that, however much time and attention he gives to the study of securities, there are thousands of others doing the same thing and many whose sources of information are superior. The opportunity to secure data does not mean that those with the best sources of information will have an advantage because of this fact. On the contrary, the opinion of officials about the prospects of the securities of their own company is rather notoriously prone to error. But it does mean that with so many eyes focused upon the financial page, while there may be many a hidden bargain which will escape attention, it is extremely unlikely that there will be any open and apparent bargains.

To illustrate this point by figures which put the matter concretely, say the bond market is at levels where bonds of medium grade are selling to yield 5 ½ per cent. A bond of this grade and in the same group which shows this yield is found to be selling at a price which will yield 7 ½ per cent. On the surface it is a bargain. The return is a full two per cent better than average for securities of the same quality. At this point it is time for the investor to pause. If it is a bargain, why have not the thousands of eyes which scan financial pages and pore over financial statistics noticed it? Is it creditable that one person, and only one, should note this exceptional situation? The answer must be that it is not credible, and from this point the next line of inquiry should be, not why this bond is a bargain, but whit is the matter with it? And in practically every case which is considered, something will be found to be the matter with it.

At the other extreme from security with the exceptionally high yield is the security, usually a stock, with an exceptionally low yield. In the case of stocks, yield is a poor yardstick. A stock selling at 150 and paying $5 in dividends is not a high income payer, but if it sells normally at between 10 and 20 times its earnings and it has an average earning power of $12 per share, there is sufficient value to sustain the price. The owner of a fixed income must measure attractiveness in terms of yield or of absolute safety. These yardsticks are not the ones, however, by which to measure the worth of equities.

8. *When low yields are a danger sign.* –But while the yardsticks for fixed-income securities ought not to be applied, as a general rule, to measure the attractiveness of equities, there are times when a low yield, by its very presence, is a warning. Suppose a corporation to have a bond issue, an issue of preferred stock and an issue of common. The bondholder is a creditor and, carrying his possible legal remedies to the last point, he can ultimately foreclose the mortgage, through appropriate legal action by the trustee, bid in the property and either completely dispossess the owners or else compel them to make a cash contribution and to accept a smaller share in the equity as the price of not being dispossessed. The preferred shareholder has no such rights but he is entailed to dividends before any are paid on the common and, in the event of liquidation of the business, his claim also ranks ahead of the common stockholder. Putting these positions in terms of risk, the bondholder has very little, the preferred shareholder more in degree, and the common shareholder is that bearer ultimately of the highest degree of risk. Now, suppose a market to have reached the boiling stage and running over the prices of security, the bonds are found to be selling at a figure which shows a yield of 5 ½ per cent, the preferred stock a price which yields 6 per cent, and the common stock at a price on which the yield from the going dividend rate is 2 per cent. Here is clearly an anomalous situation. The common shareholder, who has the greatest risk of any class of security holder, is receiving less in the way of income return than the bondholder who has very little, if any, risk.

This situation, which is not uncommon near the crest of bull markets, is one to give pause. Why put up money to purchase an income of 2 per cent when, with less money, an income of 5 ½ per cent, with much greater safety, can be obtained? The answer must clearly be that there is no logic in the proposition and the situation in itself suggests that the bonds are the better buy. Within reason, the principle remains that yield is not a yardstick for equity investments, but at periods when a yield declines well below that whish is available on senior securities of the same company, it becomes the red light of danger.

9. *Averaging purchases.* –Few policies are more prevalent than that of averaging. As it is usually practiced, an investor buys a stock at 70, presumably in the belief that it is a bargain or at least a good investment at that price. He must believe also that the trend of the market is upward, or at least that it is lateral. The instead of remaining firm or advancing, declines, either by itself or in line with a general market reaction. When the stock bought at 70 is selling at 50 the average policy is likely to be brought into play. The argument, if an averageur went through an argument with himself, would be that if the stock was a good buy at 70 it must be a much better on at 50. As far as it goes this agreement is all right, but it leaves several important matters out of the question.

In the first place, the stock may not have been a good buy at 70 and it may not be a good one even twenty points lower. The argument for averaging has no weight unless the premise that the security was an excellent buy at the first price is valid. In the second place, although the security may be reasonably worth 70, if a general market decline is in progress and no signs of the completion of that movement have appeared, there is no assurance that 50 is going to be as low a price as the issue will reach. It will be as responsive to the market trend in the future as it has been in the past and, if the bear market persists, the issue was as likely to be found some months hence selling at 30 as at 50 or more,

But, finally, there is one pertinent question which is hardly ever considered in connection with the question of averaging. The stock may have been an excellent purchase at 70 –the first question can be answered satisfactorily. The bear market may be showing good evidence of having a run its course –the second question is answered satisfactorily. Now –is the stock which was bought at 70 the best purchase now? Unless the third question can likewise be answered in the affirmative, the investor ought not to average his purchase but instead put his new funds into whatever appears, at the time, to be a better investment. This method is averaging on the market rather than averaging on the individual security. The policy for averaging has been given in some detail but it can be summed up in one sentence:

Do not buy more of a stock which you already own and have bought at a higher price unless it would be bought now on its merits, apart entirely for the fact that it is already owned.

10. *Objective and subjective approach.* –An investor needs to cultivate a purely objective approach to the whole matter of buying and selling. Assuming that sufficient attention is given to the analysis of securities and of the market, the investor will do well to truck the facts. He will do well also to distrust mere opinions, beliefs or guesses. In general, when an investor feels the greatest confidence in his position (which will generally be after he has accumulated a large actual or paper profit) it is a good time to test himself to the extent of asking how much of the confidence is based on statistics and how much on hope or the contagion of mass optimism. At the other end of the cycle, when losses have been taken or have run up on paper, it is similarly a time for subjecting discouragement and pessimism to the same test.

11. *Patience.* –There are few fields of human endeavor where the rewards of patience are so great and so tangible, and where impatience is punished so unvaryingly, as in the field of investment. One of the adages of Wall Street, already quoted, is that "The market is always here tomorrow." This is an epitome of patience and policy. If the opportunities of yesterday have been missed, the proper answer is not vain regret but, "What of it?" The market will be here tomorrow and, with it, new opportunities. If mistakes have been made in the past, the market will be here tomorrow for their correction. If a security has been bought and it shows little signs of progress in a rising market, that fact alone maybe an excellent argument against losing patience and getting rid of it. The impatient investor may be parting with a well-chosen stock in an industry which is having a late response, or which has been passed over for more active leaders just when it is about to stage its belated recovery.

12. *Past Experience.* –Records and statistics of the past are invaluable guides as precedents and as the basis for statistical analysis of securities. But what the individual investor did, or did not do, in the past is water over the dam except as it may be utilized for better action in the future. Not one cent of profit can be made in regretting past errors. Errors of judgment occur in every line of economic activity. The merchant stocks slow-selling lines; he overstocks and understocks; the manufacturer misjudges demand and finds that production schedules have been in error. When such mistakes occur, merchant and manufacturer start to clear out the excess inventories. Whether investment errors have been of omission or commission, they should be remembered only as guides to future action. Above everything, an investor should spare himself wishing and repining over what might have been done in markets of yesterday.

Advisory 2

The Market Place

1. *The investor's interest in the market.* –One of the more generally accepted lines of demarcation between the speculator and the investor is that the former is interested primarily in the movement of prices while the latter is interested primarily in values. The distinction may be accepted but it does not mean that an investor should, or can, afford to be inattentive to the minutiae of the market. Obviously one who is investing rather than trading will give less attention to minor price fluctuations in buying or selling, and, just as obviously, he will be less concerned with hour-to-hour or even with day-to-day fluctuations in price.

   But in whatever capacity one is interested in securities, some of the major features of the behavior of the market itself cannot be put aside as of minor consequence. Bearing in mind that fact that the price paid for a purchase and the price realized on a sale are both highly important parts of an investment as well as of a speculative transaction, we may outline here some of the distinguishing characteristics of market action.

2. *The message conveyed by volume.* –In dealing with the significance of the volume of trading on the stock exchange, it is unnecessary to do more than consider the significance of its implication at two extremes –one when the volume of trading is very heavy and the other when it is very light. As a preliminary, the perfectly obvious fact must be noted (because not infrequently is seems to be forgotten) that every transaction has two parties. One of the most familiar headlines on financial pages in a strong

market is that "Stocks Advance on Heavy Buying." This is undoubtedly so –but it is equally true that they are advancing on a dearth of selling. If the anxiety of persons owning stocks to sell were as great as that of the persons doing the bidding, so that offerings at the market precisely offset bids at the market, the market would not be advancing at all –it would be standing still.

Conversely, the reader of stock- or commodity- market news cannot fail to note the frequency with which stocks, or wheat, or cotton "decline on liquidation." This statement also is unquestionably true but if there were a buying demand equal in financial strength and in desire to the offerings of those doing the liquidating, prices would not be declining. Again it would be a stand-still market.

3. *The two sides of the market.* –The significance of these facts for investor and speculator alike is that with the market always a bilateral affair, attention is often given to the wrong side. The direction of the price movement is determined neither by buying nor selling, each by itself, but by which side is backed by the greater financial resources and which is stimulated by the greater urgency. When prices drop precipitately from a level which has been maintained for some time it is never an opportune time for quick action in buying. The reason is that the greatest urgency for action in such a market is that of those who are carrying securities on borrowed funds. These embarrassed owners range all the way from small shoestring speculators to operators who trade in thousands of shares, and to large financial houses which may be carrying undistributed securities. Some selling will be necessitous as loans are called, and some may be voluntary as those who are long decide that prudence is the better part of valor. But whatever the motivation and whether the action is voluntary or involuntary, the pressure is coming from sellers.

At the other extreme, after loans have gone through a long period of severe liquidation, selling pressure is largely removed. The greater urgency than is likely to be that of buyers, both large and small, who see securities selling at a bargain levels and have the resources to make their demand effective.

4. *High volume and rising prices.* –The mere fact that the volume of trading increases a prices rise need occasion no particular concern to an investor. It is a normal phenomenon for volume to rise with prices and to fall away with a price decline. In the one case the greater urgency is that of the prospective buyers, while in the other, after necessitous and policy liquidation has been completed, there is little urgency from either side. The danger-mark for the investor is when, with a large volume of trading continuing, prices fail to advance.

No better illustration of the significance of this condition to a veteran market operator can be found than in an occurrence of some years ago. The operator had wired his New York representative to add to a line of commodity then quite large, which the operator was carrying for an advance. In the place of confirmation of the carrying out of his instructions he received a brief reply at the end of the day: "Tremendous volume today but only a fractional advance in prices." The operator saw from the ten words what his New York representative had see _cancelled his buying order, unloaded his long position and went short –to his ultimate very large profit.

An investor will find the same clue of value and for the same reason. If, after an advance, a point is reached where the same large volume that has been moving prices upward cannot budge them another inch, what is happening is that selling pressure and a diminution of strength on the buying side –with the inevitable result.

5. *High volume and falling prices.* –When a bull market is breaking up and the first signs of panic appear, the volume accompanying the fall in prices will invariably be large. Witness the unprecedented and unequaled volume of the panic days of 1929 –the large volume compared with the contemporary market of the market break in the Fall of 1937. Volume rises high in a panic which is, in part, a product of necessitous selling, in part a stampede of the frightened, and in part a movement contributed to by short sellers – whose later covering operations, however, will probably bring the first signs of stability into the market.

Now, it is not the normal but the abnormal which is most useful in giving either investor or speculator a clue as to the drift of affairs. A large volume accompanying a rising market is normal –therefore it has little significance except as it may be taken as encouragement to ride with the movement and as a corroboration of the other indications that a bull market is under way. But a large volume with declining prices is abnormal. In the first place it points clearly to a predominance of selling pressure –the buyers for the time being, are completely overwhelmed. In the second place, it is not the part of prudence or common sense for people to rush to unload their possessions at ever lower prices unless a mass fear has gripped them that prices will be still lower, or unless they are compelled to take this action.

As a consequence, when prices decline to the accompaniment of a heavy volume of trading, it is a good move for investor as well as speculator to join the procession. There may be little sense in the action of a mob, or little sense in the behavior of a runaway horse, but neither can be stopped, short of overpowering or exhaustion in the latter case, or of an ebbing of the emotions which have impelled the movement in the former case. A rule to which there will be very few exceptions, and which may consequently be safely incorporated into an investment program, is to sell half, or a major part, or all of one's investments in such a period. Those held should be ones which are demonstrably cheap at prevailing prices and hence those which are reasonably certain to rebound with rapidity when the movement comes to its end.

6. *Low volume and falling prices.* –Low volume and falling prices are the normal condition in a bear market. The wholly abnormal markets of 1930 and the years following were actually not so much a bear market as a succession of panics connected by bear markets. In the average bear market, however, the tendency is for volume to recede as prices decline. The reasons for this movement are clear. Unless a vastly overextended credit situation is to be cleared up, as in 1929 and the years following, the bulk of necessitous selling usually occurs in the panic phase of a bear market –at its beginning. Those who are left long of stocks are the panic phase are for the most part people who do not have to sell.

The consequence of this condition is that offerings, instead of being poured into the market, will reach it in driblets. Here an investor may change his position by selling some securities and bury others –or he may sell some and hold part of the proceeds. Others may sell to establish tax losses. Some will come to a belated conclusion that prices are going still lower. There is always some tired-out or disappointed selling around the bottom. But none of this selling is of the urgent kind which makes for large volume. Hence –while one of the most discouraging and exasperating markets for an investor, whether he is holding securities or holding cash, is one in which prices simply drift aimlessly lower –there is nothing to fear in a trend of this sort. It is normal bear market and, before many waken to the fact, the downward drift of prices will end and they will begin to move laterally.

7. *Low volume and a lateral price movement* –Low volume of trading accompanied by a lateral price movement is the combination of volume and trend which offers the greatest opportunities to investors. It is comparatively rare thing for a market to move sidewise –the periods are short and few, studding the far more common rising and falling markets. When such a movement occurs it is a prelude to the next major or minor trend. Now suppose the lateral drift appears after a long or sharp decline. Business news at the time will be discouraging, for the bear market, of course, has preceded or run apace with a business depression. Dividends are being cut or omitted, earnings reports show greatly curtailed profits, or losses where profits used to be; newspapers are filled with news of wage cuts and lay-offs; factories are curtailing; inventories on all hands are reported excessive, and pessimism reigns. But in spite of this discouraging outlook, the market drifts aimlessly sidewise and the financial pages tell of the difficulties of the brokerage houses with business at so low an ebb.

In such a period attention is likely to be centered on the wrong side. The dull, few-hundred-thousand-share markets are cited as one more pigment touching the picture of pessimism; there is an almost total absence of buying –there is no demand –investors are hugging the sidelines. This situation may be true but it is unimportant. The important side is the selling side –there is just as evidently no selling pressure, and if, with gloom pervading the atmosphere and all surface news discouraging, there is so little stock to be dislodged, clearly the market is a stronger affair than it appears to be from its lethargic lateral drift. When months of unfavorable news will not dislodge stocks, months of unfavorable news will not dislodge stocks, they are not weakly held. Sooner or later a slight rise in demand is going to find the market practically bare of offerings and then the buying wave will start. It was from exactly such a market as this that the upward surge of prices in June, 1938, sprang.

The rule to be included in the investor's program is to buy in a laterally moving market after either a long or a sharp drop in prices and when, accompanying the lateral price movement, a practical drying up of trading has occurred.

8. *Significance of the lateral trend.* –There is more to such a side ward drift of prices, however, than the fact that the accompanying volume is low. To get at the significance from a fundamental standpoint some notice must be taken of the habits of shrewd buyers. The stock market is a great auction market. It is different in purpose, in organization and in economic function from the familiar auction room or the auction sale, but nevertheless it is an auction market. Suppose an ordinary auction to be taking place and a prospective buyer stops in to see if he can pick up some piece of furniture he needs. An inexperienced participant may be carried away by the bidding and ultimately pay more than he intends to pay possibly more than the article is really worth to him. An experienced trade representative who attends an auction, however, knows what he wants, what the articles are worth to him and how much he can pay for them and utilize them to his own profit. He will not be carried away by any amount of bidding. He will start low and go up gradually and, if the competition takes the price beyond what the articles are worth to him as a commercial proposition, he will retire.

Very much the same thing goes on in the stock-market auction market. Shrewd investors and speculators, or those with large capital who are accumulating a line of stocks to hold for an extended rise, are not going out bidding the price up on themselves. As a matter of fact they may be doing some selling while they are buying, in order to keep the price down, or to keep it from rising too fast. The accumulator of a large line of one stock or of many stocks is more likely to take what the market is offering than he is to go searching actively for the stock and so stimulate the price.

Now if buyers are sitting back and taking only what the market offers and if no urgent selling pressure exists, the direction of the price movement will be mainly lateral and its fluctuations will also be within comparatively narrow limits. In the language of the market, it may be called a trading are, or a congestion area, or a "lone" –the nomenclature is unimportant. But the nature of the movement is important. In such a market what is going on is almost invariably the transfer of stocks from weak hands to strong hands –from the financially weak, or the timorous, or the discouraged to the financially strong or courageous, or far-seeing. It is from such a foundation that some of the most rapid and spectacular market movements spring, when conditions are ripe. Hence, it is an ideal market in which to increase investment holdings.

The converse of the general proposition is true of a lateral movement after an extended rise of prices. Not all markets do slow down, but not infrequently the peak of a bull market is reached gradually. Just as a lateral movement accompanied by low volume after a long bear market is an ideal time in which to buy, a lateral trend with volume fairly high after a long rise in an excellent time for realizing profits and for a transfer of investments into mediums less volatile than common stocks.

9. *Trend lines.* –Trend lines are likely to be more a concern of active traders than of investors, but the investor cannot afford to be without a knowledge of their implications. Since price is an integral and important part of the investment operation at the time of both purchase and sale, developments in the market which give a clue to the direction of the price movement and to probable impending changes are worth noting.

If a graph of any stock market average or, for that matter, of the price movement of any one stock, is taken over a sufficiently long time –from six or eight months to a year –a general direction of the price movement will be apparent, and in that general direction there will be several upward and downward swings –intermediate moves within the main movement. Some of these peaks and valleys stand out more than others, and by laying a rule under successive bottoms points and over successive tops, there can be drean lines which are either parallel or converging.

If the lies are parallel, they indicate that sides of that path, so to speak, which the market is treading. The action of significance when such a path is being followed is a deviation from the lines which thus border its course. When the market is rising, a breaking of these trend lines on the upper side is not of particular moment. At the most it may indicate that the pace of the advance is increasing; at the least it is without significance if the market shortly afterward relapses to its former course.

But here, as in the case of volume and every other market phenomenon, it is the unusual and unexpected, rather than the regular course of action, which is significant. If the market, either abruptly or gradually breaks through the trend lines on the lower side, there is a clear warning of two things. At the least, the pace of the advance is slackening –with another low point established lower that the trend line, the slant of that line upward will thereafter be less steep. At the worst, the breaking of a trend line on the downward side may be the forerunner of the end of a movement. Whatever the subsequent course of the market may be, the action is sufficiently cautionary to warrant steps being taken at once to turn some part of the investment portfolio into cash if the turn proves to be at hand.

Trend lines which are converging instead of running parallel tell a different story. A trading area or "line" not infrequently shows this convergence. Here the market is moving, with successive upward and downward variations, toward a point, but with the extent of the minor movement constantly narrowing. Low volume characterizes such a trend and, as stock prices approach the point of convergence, fluctuations become so narrow that little movement is apparent on a chart. The direction of a breakaway of the price trend from such a convergence of trend lines is of the greatest consequence. In the vast majority of cases the direction of the breakaway will prove to be the direction of the next price trend. The trend has been in the making and hence the breaking of a converging trend line on the upper side may be taken a confirmatory of others bullish indicators, or even as a forecaster of them, while a breakaway on the down side is a warning to lighten ship immediately.

10. *Gauging the end of a market movement.* –The investor, as well as the speculator, should be able to recognize the indications of either warning or encouragements which are given by the market's action after a trend either upward or downward has been in progress for some time. There is a traders' nomenclature for the peculiarities of market action at tops and bottoms with which it will be unnecessary to deal. The point is to grasp the significance of action at the extremes and be guided by the evidence of strength or weakness which is revealed.

As a preliminary, the matter relative to "lines" or trading areas should be born in mind. The market is not always going either upward or downward but it is progression in one of these directions the greater part of the time. For it to be stationary is unusual and such a lateral movement is but the preliminary to what follows. Hence we are dealing principally with movements of prices which are making headway in the direction of the movement. The inference may be clearer if the very close parallel is drawn between the market movement and the movement of a tide. Without knowing whether a tide is at ebb or is running in, an observer on a beach need not be long in doubt. A stick stuck in the sand at the limit of an incoming wave will mark its boundary. The, if succeeding waves break over the stick and a new high point is marked which is again broken there can be no question that the tide is rising. Conversely if the water fails to reach the stick which is first employed to mark the high-water point, there is clear evidence of an ebbing tide.

The action of the market at the limit of movements parallels this movement of tides. If, in a bull market, prices rise to a peak and the back away –then, when a fresh surge of buying occurs, they rise but fall short of the first peak –and repeat the process even a second time, there is enough warning of an ebb tide impending. The numbers and financial resources of buyers are inferior to the numbers or to the urgency of sellers. On the contrary, when it is a bear market and a low has been established, if prices give way on a rally but fail to penetrate the old low point, then rise still further and hang above the old lows still on a reaction, there is the strong suggestion of rising tide with its implication as to the investment policy which it is best to follow.

If prices will not continue going up to the accompaniment of the favorable news which pervades the financial atmosphere in a bull market, it is time for caution. It they will not go down in the face of the discouraging news at the bottom of bear markets, the decline is about over.

Advisory 3

Investment Analysis

1. *The Utility of standards.* –There are two extremes in the matter of investigating a security before buying it. One is the casual purchase on verbal advice, or on the acceptance of news items or sales material, without going beneath the surface; the other is becoming so involved in detailed dissection of a security that a mere mass of material takes the place of judgment. As a rule the average investor has neither the time nor the material for detailed studies. The understanding of a number of statistical tests, however, will serve one useful purpose. Data of this sort may reveal worth-while buying opportunities. But this is not their chief function. They are more useful for revealing weaknesses or danger spots not apparent in a casual examination of income statement and balance sheet. Space here does not permit of a detailed exposition, but the conclusion to be drawn from some of the ratios which are easiest to apply from material at the command of the average investor may be summarized.

2. *The current-asset ratio.* –The current-asset ratio is perhaps the most commonly understood of the various relationships indicated by the balance sheet. Total current assets divided by total current liabilities is the process by which the ratio is derived. Whether the ration for a given company is adequate, inadequate, or more than adequate, can best be best determined by checking the result against the showing of one or more companies in the same line of business.

It will not do to take some general rule of thumb, nor to compare the ration of a company in one line with that of one in a different line. A ratio which would be satisfactory for a public utility company would be entirely unsatisfactory for a merchandising company. The purpose of the test is to show the financial strength or weakness of the company, for a subnormal ratio may suggest the possible inability of the enterprise to meet its obligations in due course if income declines, while a more than adequate ration not only is a reinforcement for any favorable conclusions drawn from the earnings trend but also augurs well for the maintenance of a dividend schedule already in effect.

3. *The quick-asset ratio.* –The procedure for determining quick-asset ratios is the same as that for current-asset ratios except that, instead of using total current assets, only those which are cash or the equivalent of cash are considered. Marketable securities, together with cash, comprise the major part, or all, of quick assets. This ration has much the same usefulness and meaning as the current-asset ratio, except that, if inventories form a substantial proportion of the current-asset total, the quick asset position may give a truer picture of the financial situation.

4. *Checking earnings from the balance sheet.* –In the discussion of industrial securities, the method of deducing earnings from the balance sheet in the absence of income statements was briefly outlined. The process is of value not only in deriving earnings but also as a check on income figures, for the most minute items of revenue and expense have a bearing on the balance sheet position and, in the aggregate, the revenues and expenditures of any period are fully reflected in balance sheet changes and in the distribution of dividends. Here the matter of balance sheet analysis for this purpose may be taken up in somewhat more detail.

We may suppose balance sheets for two periods a year apart to be available but no earnings statement as yet obtainable. Were operations profitable or otherwise? The balance sheets show the principal items given in the two periods.

The items which show no chances, the investments and the mortgage, call for no comment. The reserve item does not enter into the calculation, since this should reflect the addition to the net worth of the enterprise after dividends. The items which are of importance are those which show whether the business has increased or decreased its wealth during the year. Hence it will be clear that: (a) an increase in assets or a decrease in liabilities is a gain in wealth, while (b) a decrease in assets or an increase in liabilities is representative of a decline.

The corporation is known to have paid $22,600 in dividends during the year and these must be added to the foregoing total, making $58,200 as the apparent earnings.

This illustration is extremely simplified. In the ordinary case where the method is used, both additions to the company's wealth and decreases from it will appear in the balance sheet items. If care is taken to include dividend distributions, the method will afford a fair picture of earning power in the absence of income data.

5. *Vertical analyses.* —For the purpose of bringing in clear relief the detailed progress of a company, a form of balance –sheet analysis may be employed in which the balance-sheet items or the current asset and liability items are set up in percentages instead of using the actual data. Suppose, for example, the inventory position of a company is under investigation. Inventories are part of current assets, and the current asset total for each year being compared is taken as 100. Then, for each year under comparison, the percentage of current assets which the inventory forms is computed. A trend may be revealed which would not stand out from merely scanning the actual figures.

   An inventory item of $10,000 in the balance sheet of a company with $25,000 of current assets forms 40 per cent of the total. An increase to $11,000, so stated, does not appear great. But suppose the total of current assets at the later period is $22,000. Inventories now form 50 per cent and, thus stated, the increase appears considerably greater and of more significance.

6. *Horizontal analyses.* —Just as the balance sheets of the same company for two different periods may be used in order to note trends by reducing items to a percentage basis, so a comparison between companies in the same line of business may be both clarified and simplified. Te percentages will reveal with exactness what the figures may show only approximately, and the efficiently operated and well-financed small company will make the showing which its record and position merit in comparison with a larger unit. Size, not critically examined, may obscure unpromising factors, although, other things being equal, size is an element of preference as between different enterprises.

7. *Income ratios.* —It will be clear at a glance that the actual amount of a company's earnings, taken by itself, is a meaningless figure for analytical purposes. Earnings which in dollars would be a scanty showing for a large corporation would be fabulous profits for thousands of small manufacturing and trading companies. It is not the quantity of earnings but the story they reveal of the earning power of capital invested in the business which tells whether the railroad, or utility, or store, or manufacturing plant is a profitable and growing venture, or is just holding its own or even retrogressing.

We may start this matter of income ratios with a simple example, not of a corporation but of an individual proprietor of business. He starts with a stock of goods, opens a store in a building he owns, and for the first year carries on a cash business, making $2,000 net. There is no difficulty here in deriving some income ratios. Since hi is the sole owner and his profits are subject to no prior charge, it the total of the assets with which he started amounted to $20,000, he has earned at the rate of 10 per cent on his invested capital and he has earned at the same rate on his interest or equity in the business

The larger the corporation and the number of accounts in the balance sheet which must be considered in the computation of net worth, the more difficult is the undertaking, but it is one simply of computation. Calculation of the book value of a stock which is under consideration will show the equity of each share in the enterprise. Then if earnings are reduced to a per-share basis, the ratio of net earnings to net worth is simply the percentage which earnings per-share form of book value per share. Or net earnings and total book value applicable to the common stock may be taken without reduction to t per-share basis. Then, to derive the ratio of net income to invested capital, the total of all securities ahead of the common stock – preferred issues, if any, and bonds, if any may be added to the common and the relationship of net earnings to this figure will give a fair picture of the earning power of the company on its invested capital.

In the interpretation of this figure business conditions must be considered. A declining ratio which is a product of the times rather than something peculiar to the one enterprise modifies unfavorable implications from declining ratios. The persistence of a declining trend, even at a moderate rate, over a number of years, however, should carry its own suggestion either in regard to the entire field of business in which the company operates or in regard to the particular company.

8. *Analysis of a manufacturing company's income ratio.* –The story told by the relationship of net income to fixed assets over a term of years may be more precise. Suppose we have under examination the record of a manufacturing company which, five years ago, had a plant investment of $22,070. This item shows an increase to $25,125 the following year, then a further gain to $27,157. The next year the fixed asset investment appears as $43,875 and for the latest year for which data are available it stands at $70,810. The company has not merged with another nor absorbed another. The very considerable increase in fixed assets shown by the figures for the latest two years is evidently a reflection of a material expansion in plant facilities which have been enlarged in the quest of a greater volume of business and, presumably, of greater profits.

Turning to the record of earnings, suppose it is found that, in the earliest of these years, the company showed a net income of $18,107. In the following year it earned $20,010 and in the third year earnings were $20,182. We may ask, at this point, what is the record indicating? The earnings of the earliest year were under examination were equivalent to 82.0 per cent of the fixed assets and for the second year they were equal to 79.6 per cent. The third year shows earnings at the rate of 74.3 per cent on the company's plant account. The earnings have gained in each year but at a rate which has not equaled the increased investment in plant and machinery.

Now for the fourth year, when the plant account showed the large increase from $27,157 to $43,875, earnings amounted to $32,590. This is an increase of more than 50 per cent over the earnings of the best previous year and on the surface it appears a gratifying fixed assets increased more than 50 per cent, and despite the large gains in earnings, they were a the rate of only 72 per cent of plant value as compared with 74.3 per cent the previous year. During the last year under review earnings amounted to $48,150, which is two and two-thirds times as great as the earnings for four years before –again in apparently good showing. But compared with the increased investment in fixed assets, the record earnings were only 68 per cent –the lowest ratio for the five year period.

The prospective investor, making a superficial examination directed to the earnings record, would be impressed with the material expansion in so short a time. But when this record is compared with the sums which have been spent in enlarging the plant, it appears that the expansion has not brought in the same rate of return as formerly. Unless the drop in the ration of earnings to the plant account can be accounted for by a trend of general business, the inference must be that here expansion has been too rapid. The converse would hold true, of course, if the record showed a rate of earnings gain greater than the extent of increase in the plant account. The story would be of an expansion which was still within the bounds of the market's ability to absorb the product, or to absorb it with no increase in expense out of proportion to the gain in gross revenues.

Instances of rapid or sudden expansion ought to be submitted to an examination such as this. It is true that many corporations have grown and prospered through the policy of plowing earnings back into property, but it is by no means true that all earnings plowed back into properties yield an adequate return, or a return commensurate with the earnings on the plant before expansion. If capital was needed in the past, the plowing back of earnings proved one of the cheapest ways of acquiring it, and hence a desirable corporate policy. But if expansion is not needed, then earnings put back into property may be dissipated quite as readily as if taken out of the business entirely.

Conclusions drawn from one ratio may be checked against other ratios. In the case just considered the total of current assets and the working capital of the company for the several years in question.

Comparing an earning with this data, we see that a company was earning at the rate of 47 per cent on its current assets for the first year, 41 per cent for the second year, 37 per cent for the third year, 32 per cent for the fourth year, and 89 per cent in the latest year. Up to the last year the record of earnings on current assets tells the same story as the ratio of earnings on fixed assets. If the one shows a condition of over-expansion, the other shows that it has been impossible for the management to operate as efficiently as in the earlier years –and the same trend would appear if the comparison were made with working capital rather than with current assets.

9. *The dividend ratio.* –Objectives in the minds of investors are usually a compound of desire to conserve capital, to obtain appreciation, and to derive an income from the investment. But not infrequently an issue is bought with the expectation of a stated or regular income and shortly thereafter the dividend rate is changed. In considering the possible income from investments, emphasis should be laid not on what the corporation is paying at the time, particularly if earnings happen to be exceptionally large, but on what proportion of earnings experience shows a corporation in that line of business may be expected to pay out in dividends, year after year.

As in the case of the price-earnings ratio, this dividend ratio should be considered as an individual matter and no reliance should be placed on general rules or approximations. The tendency is for dividend payments to run higher relative to earnings for companies whose earnings show little variation from year to year than they run for companies which are in lines of business known as feast or famine.

The applicability of dividend ratios is estimating the income potentialities of a common stock for the ea4rnings and dividends for leading chemical companies for a ten-year period prior to 1935. The investor who, in 1933, considered buying into the chemical group, partly in anticipation of recovery and partly for income in the period of revival, might have noted the records.

Ratios such as these will not be a precise guide, of course, as to dividend policy anymore than other ratios are precise. Applied within broad limits, however, they are useful. If a company which has been earning at the rate of $10 per share and paying $8 per share seems likely to revert to an earnings level of $7 or $8 per share it must be assumed that, barring dirtr5ibutions out of surplus, the dividend will not be long in undergoing revision to approximately the same proportion as that of the lower earnings.

10. *Sales ratios.* –For merchandising companies in particular, data on the turnover of inventories has its usual interest. This turnover may be calculated according to the regular methods when sales figures are available. IN some instances, however, the first figurer will be gross income and when this is the case an approximation of turnover may be obtained by substituting the gross income figure for the sales figure.

When sales figures are available, or, in their absence, when gross income is given, a question bearing on the efficiency and profitableness of operations will be the number of dollars of sales or of gross income which are saved for debt service, if any, or for the shareholders. A comparison of income before fixed changes and interest, if any, taken over a sufficient number of years to be representative, will give the trend. The item so derived pictures whether the enterprise is conducting its operations efficiently, or is operation in a field which is showing steadily better or steadily diminishing results. In the case of a capital structure with no funded debt and a company with no short-term borrowing, net income will tell the same story.

11. *Inventories and current assets.* –Inventories comprise part of the current assets of a business but, while current, they are not quick. The proportion they bear to the total of current assets will carry its own suggestion of prospects. In cases where the proportion of inventories to cash and other quick assets shows a marked gain, it will usually be a reflection of slow sales. Persistence of the condition suggests the possibility of trouble from decreasing liquidity of the enterprise.

12. *Interest and fixed-charge coverage.* –the safety ore precariousness of interest and fixed-charge requirements is more often than not stated in terms of the number of times these requirements have been covered. Thus, a corporation earning $1,000,000 before interested and charges, and having a $300,000 of such obligations to meet, would be covering its requirements 3.33 times. Another way of stating precisely the same thing may be met with on occasion in financial literature. Thus, in the foregoing case, we could say that the factor of safety was 233.33 per cent of the sum required for those charges. The factor of safety is, then, simply the ratio which the surplus after interest and charges bears to the amount of charges and it is clearly the same thing as stating the coverage in terms of times earned.

Advisory 4

Public Utilities

1. *Divisions of the Industry.* –In the broadest sense, a public utility company is one whose business is the supplying of a service, or services, to all customers who may require the service, provided it is within the ability of the corporation, and provided the customer complies with reasonable regulations, which include payment of established rates. It will be apparent that this definition is broad enough to include railroads, electric light and power companies, gas companies, and local or interurban street, underground, or elevated systems of transportation. It is equally clear that it excludes the rendering of services to selected customers as compared with the public at large, and that it excludes any business which is essentially the vending of a commodity.

Both inclusions and exclusions are correct. Railroads are public utilities in the nature of their service and in the economic laws which affect their operations. If railroads and other public utilities had developed together, possibly all might have been included under on term. But the railroads were a large and, until this century was well under way, the largest single group of corporations whose securities were dealt in on organized markets. The stock market of forty years ago was largely a railroad stock market. Hence, railroads are customarily considered as a separate group, despite their proper inclusion with public utilities.

The definition of the term "public utility" definitely excludes any service which is essentially private rather than public, or which is a matter of trade more than of service. The coal dealer, or the oil company which services office and apartment buildings and residences, is performing a service, but that service is an incident in the vending of the commodity. The dividing line at this end of the field is whether the operation of a company is primarily service, or primarily sale with service as an incident of delivery.

As the term is ordinarily used, public utility companies comprise: (a) Those which supply a public service or transport, (b) Those which supply a public service of light, heat and power and (c) Those which supply a public service of communication.

Excluding the rails, in conformity with established usage, corporations engaged in activities of the above descriptions are public utilities. A company which is not so engaged is an industrial.

2. *Economic characteristics of the industry.* –Whatever the field of its operations, a public utility has a heavy investment in fixed assets. It is under an obligation to provide adequate service. This means that a transportation company must run its trains or vehicles to take care of the few travelers in off hours as well as the many travelers in rush hours. The lighting company must be able to take care of the maximum needs of the community at the times when that need is greatest, and the requirement has the disadvantage that at hours and seasons of less than peak demand the plant is not utilized to capacity. Furthermore, a utility must look to the future. Facilities cannot be provided overnight, and it is necessary to plan ahead so that capacity may always be adequate, and hence always ahead of the normal growth of the community. Investment in fixed assets bulks large among the assets of the utility, and, in the proportion of fixed assets to total, lies of the lines of demarcation between utility and industrial.

To illustrate, a progression may be noted. To begin with one of the large financing companies, the statement shows no fixed assets at all. Its property consists entirely of cash, receivables, investments, furniture and fixtures, some repossession, and miscellaneous items. A merchandise company has its principal investment in current items, of which the inventory is one of the largest divisions. Progression further, we find that one of the largest industrial companies in the chemical group has 55.3 per cent of its assets represented by the fixed-property account, and still further up in the proportion of fixed assets we find a large Oil company, premier domestic unit in this extractive industry, with $1,078,000,000 of fixed assets out of $2,071,000,000 total, the properties, plant equipment and patents comprising 52 per cent of all assets.

But compare this with one of the large operation units in the electric light and power field. Out of $724,000,000 total assets, the corporation's plant accounts for 56 per cent, while, when advances to subsidiaries and affiliate companies are taken, together with the plant account approximately 85 per cent of assets are apparently of fixed character, either directly owned or represented by investment.

As a consequence of the heavy proportionate investment in fixed assets, costs are rigid. Taking the consolidated income of the same utility for a representative year, gross income from operations amounted to $155,000,000. Fixed charges absorbed some $12,000,000 of this, an item which is not subject to ready reduction. Operation expenses amounted to $114,000,000, and these expenses include taxes, maintenance, depreciation, costs of operation, which cover wages, fuels and materials, and power purchased.

Of these items the following may be said: clearly taxes are not subject to change with the volume of business; maintenance cannot be skimped without results being reflected in inadequacy of service, increased costs of increased capital investment later, or all; depreciation cannot be reduced below a reasonable amount without an overvaluation of the assets, deceptive to shareholder and rate-payer; and, since plants must be kept in operation, the reduction of fuel, material and wage costs is possible only within the narrowest of limits.

Since costs are thus rigid, the public utility industry, like the railroad industry, is one subject to the economic rule of increasing returns. In a period of expanding consumption, the point is reached where revenue increases faster than the increase in costs, and the utilities then enjoy their periods of prosperity. When revenues are declining, on the other hand, and the rate of decline exceeds the rate of reduction of costs, companies in the industry meet with their most difficult periods.

3. *Capital structure of utilities.* –The proportionately large investment in fixed assets makes for a characteristic capital structure for public utility companies. The physical equipment is fixed, it is of relatively long life, and revenues are relatively stable. The industry is able, accordingly, to finance with a considerably larger proportion of bonds and preferred stocks than would be possible, or desirable even if possible, for an industrial company. Taking another large company of illustration of capital structure is found to consist of $144,320,000 of funded debit and approximately $130,000,000 of capital stock, and almost even division, but with the bonds predominating. Other utilities have not only a substantial proportion of their capital represented by borrowed funds, but by one or more issues of preferred stock as well. Consolidations of two large companies in neighboring service areas are

instance of premier utilities with these classes of fixed-income securities ahead of their common stock.

The combination of increasing returns and this form of capital structure makes the utilities subject to rather wide variations of earning power, despite the fact that revenues, as compared with those of industrial companies, are relatively stable.

The steadiness of the relationship between operating expenses, including taxes, and gross revenues in which the operating ratios of two leading operating units in the electrical field are given for a seven-year period. Note that in seven years, which included a period of depression and a period of active business, the operating expenses, including taxes are not below 65.81 per cent gross, nor above 68.70 per cent, a variation of less than 3 per cent of revenues. The other company showed a slightly wider range, with 59.8 per cent at the highest ratio and 55.2 per cent as the lowest, a variation of over 4 ½ per cent of gross.

As against this stability for the electrical companies, gas companies tell a very simple cyclical difficulties of the gas companies. Operating expenses are steady, relative to revenues, for the last four years of a period with a wide increase in costs is apparent in transition from the depression, when commodity prices were low, to the period of active business and higher prices. The greater variation for gas companies is characteristic of the business, and marks securities of manufacturing gas companies unsuitable for investment in a period of marked prolonged, or rapidly rising commodity prices. In a period such as that which followed the World War when all prices were height, the condition which spelled prosperity for many industrials marked a period of the lowest earning for gas companies in many years.

The moderate variations in gross revenues are accentuated, first, by the rigid cost factor and, secondly by the capital structure, so that when finally translated into earnings per common share, the change from a year of prosperity to one of depression is of considerably more consequence to the investor than the mere variation in revenue would indicate.

4. *Aspects of public regulation.* –The nature of the business of public service corporations brings them under state regulations. They perform services which are essential to their communities –so essential that, just as a railroad must provide service, regardless of its financial condition, its relations with connecting carriers and the public, or the desires of its management, so that public utility is under regulation as to the rates it may charge and other phases of the services it provides.

Without touching upon the legal questions involved in the various bases which have been established for regulation, it may be said that the aim of regulation is generally to insure to that consumer a fair and reasonable charge, which, at the same time, is sufficient to enable the company to earn at a rate which will enable it to maintain its properties and services efficiently operation, and to provide a fair return on the investment which the property represents. It must be understood that the term "return on the investment" does no refer to the rates on particular securities, although these may be taken into account. Rates may be authorized with a view to enabling a utility to maintain a dividend rate which is regarded as fair, on its stock outstanding. But fundamentally, the rate of return relates to the earnings of the invested capital, and thus relates to the sum of assets rather than to the interest or dividends on different classes of securities.

It will be evident that, at this point, another important question arises which is a complement of the rate question. Before deciding what rate a company should be permitted to earn on its investment, the value of that investment is first to be ascertained. The valuation of the properties on which rates are calculated is known as the rate base. It is the starting point for the determination of reasonable charges.

Rate regulation, then, looks to physical values and to the charges based on those values. With the utilities, as a whit the railroads, a peculiar delusion appears to pervade the minds of investors or speculators on the matter of rates. An increase in rates is practically always regarded as a favorable development, and prices of securities advance. A decrease in rates is regarded as unfavorable. If, in any case, rate decreases were carried to a point where operations could not be conducted with any profit, or where losses were inevitable, the low rates would be a bear argument. But this eventuality is beside the point, since it is as much the function of regulatory bodies to adjust rates so as to insure at least the solvency of utilities, as it is to adjust them in the interests of the consumer.

Granting the point that there are levels below which rates cannot go without impairing the position of utilities, it must be observed that ample remedy exists at law if this point is ever reached. For the kind of rate reduction encountered is practice, however, the implication need not be bearish. In a period when the demand for the utility's services is expanding, it may be, as a matter of fact, somewhat favorable. It will be so to the extent that the lower rate stimulates additional use of the utility's services.

5. *The trend of rates.* —Single instances of rate reductions, then, need have no unfavorable connotation. Looking to trends, however, it must be apparent that the course of rates is more likely to be downward rather than upward, and when

adjustments are made upward in periods of rising costs, the advance in rates I likely to lag considerably behind the advance in costs. Except in the case of marked cost advances, resistance to rate increases is always strong. Consumers are much more numerous than public utility shareholders, officers and employees, and the numbers interested in lower rates will always be greater than the numbers instead in advances. And while single instances of rate reduction may be favorable rather than unfavorable at a given time, a continued trend downward for the selling price of any commodity ore service is a factor militating against the attractiveness of the industry as a long-pull investment medium.

While the trend of rates is more likely to decline, in the long run, than to advance, or even to remain stable, the prospect of the industry is reasonably favorable for further extensive growth. More than half of the business of the utilities proceeds from wholesale rather than retail use, including in this category manufacturing industries and public corporations which are consumers of electrical energy. The industry is alert, also in the development of new uses, and it is improbable that the full extent of development has been reached.

But, of the foregoing avenues of development, only the sales to new customers and for new purposes are extensive developments. Where the use of energy in territory already covered is increased, as by the development of new uses and new appliances, the growth of the business is intensive and the stage of intensive development represents the second, or maturity, period in the life of an industry, as the extensive development stage represents the pioneer period. In this respect, the life of an industry resembles that of a country newly settled. For the greater part of the Nineteenth Century, the growth of the United States was extensive. Then the time arrived when the frontier disappeared –and from that time the problems became increasingly those of a more mature state of development.

A further problem faced in utility growth is that of competition and substitution. Privately operated Diesel plants make some encroachment on the industrial consumption of energy. Gas, as a fuel encounters the competition of oil.

If some of the limitations of the utilities as investment mediums have been indicated, it has been simply to present a realistic picture of the situation. It is not to inferred that, where extensive growth is replaced by intensive growth, improvement ceases. What is more likely is a slowing down of the rate at which growth has proceeded.

6. *Elements of operating costs.* –In the divisions of operating costs the breakdown is given in general terms. Precise percentages naturally vary from year to year, and

from period to period. For the purpose of an outline of the relationship of operating costs to the investment position of the utilities, the use of round figures is sufficient.

In round numbers, then, some 60 per cent of the dollar which the utility takes in revenue is expended in cost of operation. Of the major divisions of costs, depreciation, taxes and collections take a prominent place, consuming somewhat more than 40 per cent of the total operating costs. The items, such as depreciation and taxes, it will be noted, are inflexible, that is, not subject to change in accordance with fluctuations in revenue. Depreciation goes on regardless of business, and a skimping of allowance at one time for an industry must be compensated for later. Since depreciation charges relate to the value of properties, and since the latter form the base of which h rates are levied, it is apparent, also that regulatory bodies are concerned directly with the adequacy of depreciation charges.

Next to these inflexible items, salaries and wages take the largest part of the utilities' expenditures for operation. The item is more flexible than that of taxes, but clearly within definite limits. Service cannot be impaired, and the flexibility of costs through reduction in the personnel, or in the payroll, is circumscribed rather narrowly. Fuel costs are likely to run somewhat above ton or eleven per cent. This item fluctuates with major changes in commodity prices, but the variation from year to year is not ordinarily great. At a time of extensive price rises for commodities in general, fuel costs may increase to an extent which encroaches heavily on profits. The period of war and post-war inflation, for example seriously curtailed the earning power of manufacturing gas companies, for which the fuel item bulks relatively large. The maintenance costs, which run somewhat under ten per cent, are ageing comparatively rigid.

7. *Operating ratios.* –For public utilities, as for railroads, the operation ration is an important indicator of comparative profitableness as between different companies. It is of less use in comparing the results of one period with those of another, for while costs are relatively inflexible, the changes which general influences, such as fluctuations in commodity prices, produce may unduly raise the ratio at one period, and contribute to an artificially or superficially unfavorable comparison with another when the general price level was lower.

Among the major divisions of operating utilities, hydro-electric plants are normally found to have the lowest operating ratios, with costs fluctuation around 50 per cent of revenues. Steam plants have a normally higher ratio, the lowest ratios for this class comparing approximately with the highest for hydro-electric plants. For manufacturing gas companies, the ratio is likely to be higher than for either class of electric power producers.

31

For the purposes of detailed and intensive study of operating utilities, a variety of data are available. The average investor is perhaps best served by concentrating on a few series which are available for different purposes. For electric companies the capacity to serve the territory is measured by the installed capacity in terms of kilowatts per 1,000 inhabitants, and the number of meters per 100 or 1,000 inhabitants, or per mile of main, is a measure of the availability or utilization of the service.

8. *Capitalization of public utilities.* –The nature of the public utility business, with its large investment in plant and equipment, proscribes, in a measure, the form which capitalization must take. Borrowed capital plays a prominent part in utility financing and since the life of assets is long, the major part of borrowed capital is represented ordinarily by funded debt.

But while bonds bulk large in the securities structure of practically all utilities, a wide gap may exist between the capitalization of a local operating company and that of a holding company which has carried trading on the equity to a point as far as the equity may be made to stretch. A holding company is far from being characterized, however, by an attenuated capital structure. While this form of organization lends itself to a piling up debt, with all the accompanying financial risks, numerous examples of holding companies with exceedingly conservative capital structures can be found.

Stated in the most simple form, the borrowed funds of a utility, like those of an industrial company or of a n individual, should bear some reasonable and standard relationship to the assets it owns, and to the earnings from which interest on the borrowed funds is to be paid. The one forms the last bulwark of safety for the lenders and the other is the measure of the company's ability to carry on without encountering difficulties which would contain the possibility of its passing into the hands of a receiver.

An investor examining a balance sheet to determine the capital set-up, with an eye solely to the capital structure as of a given year, would have found major divisions of the balance sheet carrying the totals shown.

First, how does this structure appear from the standpoint of bondholders? The resources total more than $250,000,000 and the funded debt amounts to slightly less than $70,000,000. There are more than $3.50 of assets for every dollar of funded debt, and this may be regarded as excellent security for the bonds of such a company. A fair general rule for estimating the conservatism of the debt structure is to borrow a standard from the real estate field, where a mortgage which is not subject to amortization is regarded as conservative if it does not exceed 50 per cent of the value of the property-two dollars of property for one dollar of the mortgage debt.

A second direction for inquiry is the relationship of the funded debt to the company's net worth or stockholders' equity. The equity is represented by the stock capitalization, which totals $91,834,715, and the paid-in and earned surplus. These surplus accounts combined with the capital stock give an equity of $139,480,181. The funded debt is approximately half of this amount, a ratio which may be taken as a perfectly conservative. Taking a parallel from the real estate field, the situation resembles that of a $100,000 house with a mortgage of approximately $3,300.

9. *Relationship between earnings and capitalization.* –Of more immediate importance than the asset protection for security holders is the adequacy of earning power. Earning power obviously bears a direct relationship to capitalization. Earnings can carry only so much of a load. The load may be increased with reasonable safety within definite limits, but an indefinite extension of the burden on earnings means ultimate collapse at the first unfavorable turn in the trend. Viewed in another way, earning power may be taken as the foundation which will support a properly built capital structure, but which will cave in if the superstructure is too heavy for the foundation.

For the year of the balance sheet shoes gross earnings of $41,050,0000, and $10,203,000 was available for fixed charges. Interest requirements totaled $4,660,000 so that requirements were being covered more than 2 ¼ times. This amount may be taken as a reasonable minimum coverage for fixed-charge requirements. Preferred dividends required $804,000 making combined fixed charges and preferred stock dividends of $5,464,000. The earnings available were close to twice this amount and here, again, the fair minimum was met.

In practice, one year ought never to be the basis of determination either of a security's presumed attractiveness or of its weakness. The data taken are sufficient to illustrate the point but, in practice, a period of not less than five, and preferably one of seven to ten years is needed. The period should be sufficiently long to include a record of performance under both favoring and adverse conditions.

Another yardstick for the analysis of utilities, considering the relationship between earnings and capitalization, is the ratio of gross revenue to capital. Gross earnings for the year in question were $ 41,058,000. Capital stock totaled $91,835,000 (including common and preferred), or a little less than 2 ¼ ties the operation

33

revenues of all subsidiaries. Combined bonds and stock of the consolidated system were somewhat less than four times gross earnings.

10. *Capital structure of utilities.* –the comparative rigidity of costs makes for a natural leverage in utility companies –that is, a drop in revenues is reflected by a larger proportionate decline in net income, while a rising trend of revenue means a greater proportionate gain in net income. To this natural leverage, the characteristic capital structure, with a large proportion of bonds, adds another or double leverage. The existence of the double leverage favors concentrating on companies whose capital st4ructures are not overbalanced by a load of funded debt out of proportion to the stock, or combined stocks. An illustration of a conservative set-up, with $69,081,000 of bonds and $91,835,000 of stocks. Here the ownership interest is greater than the funded debt. Another illustration of a fairly even balance with fended debt of $60,155,000 and stock issues totaling $75,000,000.

With the set-up in these companies may be contrasted the structures of some of the more attenuated holding companies of the boom era. For example, a funded debt of $208,877,000, and purchase-money obligations and notes of $16,000,000 ahead of an ownership interest represented by $12,914,000 of subsidiary preferred stocks and $85,632,000 combined preferred, Class A, and common of the parent company. The debt, funded and otherwise, was here more than double the equity represented by all classes of stock.

11. *Consolidated vs. parent-company data.* –In all cases where the securities of a holding company are under consideration, the data receiving attention should be the consolidated figures rather than those of the holding company alone. The leverage factor may magnify or depress the income figures of the parent company. Particularly where the examination is to show true earning power, the parent company figures alone may mislead. The reason for this fact is that the parent company shows, as its income, only the dividends and interest is received on the subsidiary securities it owns. But subsidiaries may have earned more than they disbursed in dividends –earnings which would thus not be reflected in the statement of the parent company alone. Reliance on the latter figures would clearly understate the earning power of the system to the extent of all subsidiary earnings in excess of dividends.

This situation may be illustrated by a holding company with a reported gross income of $4,957,782, composed of dividends and interested on the bonds, notes and stocks of subsidiaries and dividends on its stock ownership. Net income amounted to $4,399,241, which, after deduction of preferred dividends, was equivalent to $1.30 per share of common stock.

The earnings per share, therefore, as shown by the consolidated figures, were approximately 30 per cent greater than those shown by the parent company's statement alone.

Advisory 5

Industrial Stock

1. *Types of industrials.* –In a sense the term "industrial stocks" is exclusive, since it is the description generally given to all stocks which are not railroad, public utility, or finance company issues. Except for such a broad distinction, however, the term is too inclusive, for it comprehends stocks and groups of stocks of companies engaged in widely different lines of activity, and subject, in some respects, to different influences. The lines of differentiation will be clear from a brief glance a t leading companies whose shares are regarded as leaders in their several fields.

A large and important section of industry is engaged, either wholly or in part, in the extraction and sale of minerals, either to manufacturers or indirectly to consumers. The mining and oil industries are readily recalled as examples. Copper companies, lead producers and gold miners have their primary activity in the extraction of their respective metals. But while these companies are similar in the nature of their activity, they are dissimilar in their markets, for the base metal producers are producing chiefly for a manufacturers' market –they are purveyors to industry –while the gold miners are primarily purveyors to governments. By contrast with both of these divisions of the mining group, oil companies, whether producers, or producers and refiners, while engaged in an extractive industry, and while marketing much of their product to industry, find a large market for their products with the individual consumers.

The same line of differentiation with regard to type of market exists between industries when we come to manufacturers who are not engaged in the extraction of any raw materials. For example, a manufacturer of cigar and cigarette wrapping machinery has its market entirely with manufacturers. Some leading manufacturers have different market diversities between business and individuals. While cigarette manufacturers stand as caterers entirely to the individual-consumer trade. A group clearly distinguishable from the foregoing would be that of companies which purchase agricultural products and distribute them, changed in form in varying degrees, to consumers, either direct or through trade channels. A dairy producer is industrial, although they are not manufacturers in the sense of the company which fabricates a product out f a diversity of materials.

The industrial classification includes, in addition to manufacturers, companies whose activities are primarily the distribution of goods or services. Individual and chain stores are primarily merchandisers and incidentally producers; a corporation operating a fleet of taxicabs, or running warehouses, is selling services rather than goods, and is not engaged in manufacture at all. This summary of the inclusiveness of the description "industrials" suggests that, in the actual business of investing, due allowance must be made for variations in the nature of the business, and that broad rules are subject to modification. With this limitation in mind, however, some of the fundamentals may be stated.

2. *The volume of business.* –Volume of business done is of importance for the light it throws on whether an industrial corporation is maintaining its ground, growing, or losing ground. Few business enterprises hit a head level of activity and remain there for any length of time. The history of industrials is one either of growth or of retrogression. This statement does not imply that a company which is apparently losing ground need be in imminent danger of dissolution. The life of a business may extend over decades on a dwindling volume. But it is certain that a time of liquidation, voluntary or otherwise, must be the final fate of a business whose volume of business shows a decline long continued. The drop may be due to changes in public taste, to management policies, or to a failure to hold dup in competition with more progressive competitors. It may result, also, from economic changes-thee passing of old industries and the growth of new ones.

In this connection, it is the trend of earnings over a period of years, preferably long enough to include both extreme prosperity and extreme depression which should be observed. In any case, where a declining trend in the volume of business is apparent, the stock is best left alone, for, even though improvement may occur in one or more years, the recovery will apparently be simply an interruption of the trend. A second reason is that, for the long pull, and industry or a company which is not showing positive evidence of expansion is clearly undesirable.

For the purpose of comparison between companies in the same line of business and for similar periods of time, the gross revenue trend may be further noted in the revenue-producing ability of the capital invested in plant and machinery. Of two companies assumed to be engaged in the same line, A shows an average gross revenue of $27,600 and its plant investment is 127,275 while B does a gross business of $14,899 with a plant valued at $94,415. The revenue of A is equal to 21.7 per cent of its capital invested in plant and equipment, while B earns at a rate of 15.8 per cent. The comparison shows A to better of the two on the one point of business obtained for the dollar of invested capital.

It does not tell anything, of course, about the profitableness of operations, and a comparison, such as this, while valuable for the purpose above stated, must be used with care in comparing results for different periods of time, or in comparing companies engaged in different lines of business. The influence of periods of prosperity and depression affects the comparison over a period of years for the same company, whereas, as between different companies in different lines, the earning power of capital in an automobile plant, for example, has no necessary relationship to the earning power of capital in a chemical works.

3. *Operating efficiency.* –If the volume of business and its trend are of importance in appraising the position of an industrial company, the efficiency of operations is vital in determining how much of the dollar which comes to the company from its sales is preserved finally for the common share holder. For all groups, this relation of the cost of doing business to the volume of business carried on is known as the operating ratio. In the case of railroads, whose accounting methods are not so uniform, but assuming the data are sufficient, the two items and their relationship will tell a helpful and often revealing story. An illustration from the data of a machine manufacturing company will bring out the point.

The year 1920 was one of general business prosperity and the year of 1924 was one of a moderate depression. The periods stand opposed in another way, for in 1920 business was in the process of passing from prosperity to depression, while in 1924 it was beginning to emerge from dullness. In the former year, the machine manufacturing company did a gross business of $31,516,000 at a cost of

$28,012,000. Its net available for stock, was 11.2 per cent of gross, and the operating ratio 88.8 per cent. Four years later the changed conditions saw gross business of $27,686,000, a reduction from the volume of the prosperous year. But $3,221,000 of this business was preserved as net income and this was 11.6 per cent of the gross. The operating ratio, then, was 88.4 per cent. This simple comparison shows that the company had gained rather than lost in efficiency, for on a lower volume of business it was saving slightly more of each sales dollar for its shareholders than it had been able to save in the more prosperous days. Put in another way, it succeeded in reducing costs at a rate somewhat greater than the decline in gross revenue.

4. *Sources of long-term capital.* –In the case of railroads and utilities, a substantial part of the assets is represented by rails, equipment, plant, machinery and other fixed assets of comparatively long life. The revenues of both, while subject to fluctuation with the ups and downs of business are nevertheless somewhat steadier than those of industries performing services which are in less constant demand. As a consequence long-term capital is raised most cheaply by borrowing, the borrowing taking the form of bonds.

Industrial companies, however large or financially strong, are not in the same situation. The steel industry has a large investment in plant and equipment, and on this score steel companies might properly raise a portion of their capital by borrowing. But the steel industry is also known as one of the "feast or famine," meaning that its earnings are subject to such wide swings that it is either exceedingly prosperous or exceedingly depressed. This fact bears upon the long-term capital problem not only of steel companies but of all industrials.

Preferred dividends may be passed to conserve cash, and no interruption of the corporate life or management necessarily occurs, but a bond, with its definite promise to pay at maturity and to pay interest at the stipulated periods, has it s disadvantages for any business whose earnings fluctuate widely. An industry cannot count upon average earning power alone except in so far as average earnings enable it to build up its financial position. A series of poor years, finally entailing an inability to meet interest, or a difficulty over a maturity, will set average performance at naught.

As a consequence the industrial bon d is a less familiar investment instrument than that public utility or the rail bond. Merchandising enterprises practically never restore to finding their indebtedness. The most conservatively managed heavy manufacturing enterprises keep funded debt at a minimum, and usually get rid of it as the opportunity presents. A few examples will illustrate the point.

Company A entered the decade after the War with $10,000,000 of debentures and $82,000,000 of stock, divided evenly between common and preferred. The funded debt was little over 10 per cent of the capital structure but before the end of 1925 It was completely retired. Company B's capital structure in the mid-1930's contained funded debt and purchase-money obligation of roughly $120,000,000 while common and preferred stocks were $1,230,000,000. The long term debt was less than 10 per cent of all capital issues.

In the period of the early 1930's the funded debt of Company C constituted about 25 per cent of the capital structure. This proportion was raised somewhat by financing with convertible bonds in 1935, but by the end of the following year the funded debt had disappeared from the capital structure through exercise of the conversion privilege.

These illustrations show that moderate part which bonds play in the capital structure of leading and conservatively capitalized industrial companies. About 25 per cent may be taken as a far maximum. A bonded debt in excess of this should have exceptionally strong and stable earnings coupled with the first class financial condition –a combination which is not often met, since the industrial with these qualifica5ions is likely to have taken the first opportunity presented to get rid of bonds entirely, if it ever had any.

5. *Working capital: amount and composition.* There are several approaches to an inquiry about the adequacy and composition of the working capital of an industrial company. Before taking up these avenues of inquiry, some typical examples of the component elements of working capital should be set out. One company in the extractive industries, one heavy industry and one merchandising or trading company.

Differences in the composition of the current assets will be noted which may be recognized as springing from the nature of the several businesses. Company 1 metals and manufactured products account for slightly less than 60 per cent of the current asset total while the items corresponding in Company 2 heavy metal's statement amount to 68.8 per cent of current assets. Company 3, however, has more than three-quarters of its current assets represented by merchandise inventories. This is about as high a proportion as the inventory account ought to attain relative to current assets and it is found naturally for the trading company whose stock-in-trade forms a larger proportion of total assets than it does for the manufacturer, particularly the manufacturer in a heavy industry.

A study of the current asset composition over a period of years will show the representative ratio of inventories to total current assets and the study prosecuted over a number of companies in the same line will enable a fair standard to be worked out for the industry as a whole. The standards so indicated will show whether the inventory carried at any given period is exceptionally large, or is normal, or subnormal.

Two common tests applied to the relationship between current assets and liabilities are the relationship of the asset total to the liability total, generally known as the current-asset ratio, and the relationship which cash and cash equivalent bear to current liabilities, know generally as the quick-asset ratio. In the case of Company 3, cash alone is more than $5,000,000 in excess of all current liabilities, which is a sufficient test of the strength of the company's current financial condition. The current-asset ratio is the total of current assets divided by the total of current liabilities. This, in the case of Company 1, is seen to be almost exactly 5 to 1. The quick assets are represented by the cash and marketable securities. In the case of Company 1, these fall below the total current liabilities, while in the case of the merchandising company, Company 3, the ratio is better than 1 ½ to 1.

The working capital of an industrial enterprise has a relationship to the size of the enterprise as represented by the owners' investment, and to the volume of business which the corporation does. Adequacy of amount of working capital in relation to size of unit may be estimated by a comparison with capital and surplus, representing the ownership interest. For the three companies mentioned previously, Company 1's capital stock and surplus amounted to $500,000,000 and the working capital of $79,785,000 was 15.95 per cent of this amount. This ratio may be regarded as fairly standard for a producer of raw materials. Company 2 with $363,000,000 of working capital showed an ownership investment of $1,591,000,000 represented by capital and surplus, the working capital amounting to 22.84 per cent of the ownership, while for Company 3 the working capital of $50,409,000 was 25.98 per cent of the ownership interest. In both cases the ratios would be taken as approximately standard. The trading company will normally show a higher ratio than the manufacturer and the range of from 20 to 25 per cent, with merchandising companies at the upper level, gives a fair test of adequacy.

As with other items and rations, the trend of working capital and its components needs to be examined over a period of years to note whether the ratios of assets to liabilities are showing a pronounced change which may be attributable to more than accidental causes, for indications which may be afforded of trends in the composition of the assets, or as to any impairment of the position suggested by a growth of liability items such as bank loans. The working capital position bears not only on the financial situation of the company –its solvency and its ability to meet obligations or to pay dividends –but in lines where advantageous terms are gained by cash payments it may have a direct influence on earnings through the lower cost of inventory or stock-in-trade.

6. *Estimating earnings from the balance sheet.* –Comparative balance sheets may be used for estimating the earnings of corporations in cases where the latter figures are not available, or for checking the earnings shown by the income statement. The net results of a year's operations are reflected in changes in balance sheet items. If the operation has been profitable, the change in the shareholders' equity is usually represented by an increase in surplus. Losses decrease the surplus. Now, supposing no other data were available, what could be made of two balance sheets, for successive years, both of which showed the same amount of capital stock outstanding, but the latter of which showed a surplus of $96,104 as against the earlier balance sheet's $86,768? The corporation is known to have paid dividends amounting to $23,289 during the year.

The corporation has apparently added $9,336 to surplus during the year and its dividend payments totaled $23,289. We now have a set of figures which ought to reveal the corporation's earnings, for, outside of reserves which may be in excess of the purposes for which they are set up, and which therefore are, to that extent, a surplus in disguise, the balance of net income after dividends has enlarged some one or more of the corporation's assets to the extent of $9,336 and the dividends were clearly paid out of earnings. The sum of the two figures is $32,625. Now, in the absence of any other data, we should be safe in assuming that this figure represented the earnings of the corporation. In the case at hand, the verification may be supplied. The figures given above are those of successive balance sheets of Company 3 with three digits omitted. The earnings of Company 3 as so deduced were $32,625,000 and for the year in question, as net income in the income statement, less $300,000 tax on undistributed surplus.

7. *Inventory turnover.* –In cases where merchandising companies are under consideration, comparative data of inventory turnover may be of use, particularly in cross-comparisons of companies engaged in the same lines. When sales or gross revenues are available, an approximation of turnover may be made for illustration, the case of a corporation having sales of $290,387, and sales of $282,670 in another and earlier periods, may be considered. The inventories

carried at the beginning of the later year were $ 44,241 and at the end of the year they amounted to $38,676. The average inventory derived –which is really a mean of the two year-end figures, is $41,458. Dividing the $290,387 of reported sales by the mean inventory gives approximately 7 as the turnover for the establishment for the later year.

Turning to the earlier period, the company had an average, or mean, inventory of $2,115, derived in the same way by taking the average of the beginning and year-end figures. The assumed inventory divided into the reported sales of $282,670 gives 8.8. On these data the turnover in the earlier period was greater than in the more recent year. It would be necessary to consider the state of general business in both years –changes in activity might account for much of the difference. If no external factors serve to explain the drop, the stock, on this one count, will clearly be less attractive.

8. *Depreciation charges.* –While there are no set standards, depreciation rates common to different industries may be estimated by examining representative financial statements for a period of several years. Once a reasonable standard is determined either for an industry or for a company, its use is to enable variations to be checked. It is possible for instance, by depreciating plant or equipment at a comparatively low rate, for a company to make a better earnings statement than its performance should actually show. These figures shown by different companies in the same line may often be broken down with interesting results by recasting financial statements so as to apply, to all the companies under examination, the depreciation rates of the organization using the highest rate. On occasion, this test will show that some of the apparently excellent earnings performances are actually less favorable than those of other units with higher depreciation charges.

9. *Measuring the rate of earnings.* –The most common method of expressing the earning power of corporations is in terms of dollars per share earned. This method applies to corporations in all lines. In the case of industrials, however, it is slightly more complicated or likely to be, because of the more frequent changes in capitalization. Any change which increases the equity of a single share of stock, or decreases its equity in the business, is a change which must be allowed for, and adjustments must be made in the computation of earnings per share.

Corporation A has a stock capitalization of $1,000,000 represented by 10,000 shares of $100 par. It earns for four years an average of $100,000 and, for the sake of convenience, let it be assumed this is the annual earnings rate. Earnings,

43

than, are equivalent to $10 per share ($100,000 /10,000). The corporation now expands by selling 2,000 shares at a price to net par, bringing $200,000 in through the sale. The first year the new capital is at work, earnings amount to 120,000 and this is equal to $10 per share on the larger capitalization. Here no adjustment of the earnings of prior years is necessary. There is a larger stock capitalization, but a dollar of assets has been acquired for each increase of $1 in common stock capitalization –the equity of the old shareholders has been neither decreased nor increased.

Corporation B has a like capitalization and its earnings record has been the same. In the same year in which Corporation A sells 2,000 shares of stock, Corporation B declares a 20 per cent stock dividend. It earns likewise $120,000 or at the rate of $10 per share for the year in which the stock dividend was declared. In this case, to determine the average earning power per share, it is necessary to adjust the earnings of prior years. There are 12,000 shares of stock outstanding where formerly there were 10,000 shares and the equity of each share in earnings and assets has been decreased. Hence, taking the assumption with which we started, that the corporation earned at the rate of $100,000 annually, the investor analyzing the security would now divide the $100,000 earnings of prior years by 12,000, the present capitalization. He would finish with the equivalent of $8.33 per share earned for each of the previous four years on the present capitalization and, with $10 per share earned in the latest year, the average earning power is apparently $8.67 per share.

A split of stock accomplished by a change in the par value, or by changing from par to no par, calls for the same type of adjustment. Again, for illustration, a corporation earning at the rate of $10 par share on $100 par stock, changes to a no-par stock and issues two no-per shares for each $100 par share held. The average earning power of the new stock becomes $5 per share –the equity of each share in earnings and assets has been halved.

10. *The equity of shares.* –The equity which each share of stock has in earnings is shown by the calculation of earnings per share. The equity in assets is the book value. As far as the attractiveness of a stock for investment purposes is concerned, the book value figure is not significant. It will vary widely for different lines of industry. The required data are the number of shares of stock outstanding, the total book number of shares of stock outstanding, the total book value as shown by the balance sheets, and any changes in capitalization affecting the equity of shares in assets and earnings. On a book value of $195,756,000 Company X showed a book value per share of $65.81 per share book value of

the prior year is adjusted for the three-for-one split, becoming $21.49 per share on the basis of the present outstanding stock.

Advisory 6

Bank Stock

1. *Place of banks stocks in the investment portfolio.* –Not infrequently investment in a bank stock has aspects other than the one of strict analysis. Particularly in smaller communities, considerations of business, prestige, or other matters apart from cold investment analysis, enters into the question. Stocks of the large banks in financial centers such as New York, Chicago, Philadelphia, San Francisco, Boston, St. Louis and some other cities of similar size, however, have a well-organized over-the-counter market and some of them are found with fair frequency in both large and small portfolios.

   In one sense it might appear that a bank stock is an excellent two-way hedge. This characteristic will be clearer after a brief note of the bank's income sources and the conditions which favor or which work against the development of earning power. The main activities of the bank are investment and the extension of credit. It has other earning activities but the two stated are primary.

   As to a large part of its business it is like a specialized investment trust, with its field of activity circumscribed by law, and by the policies of its management, to investment with a view at all times to liquidity and stability. This status means that the quality of a banks investments are normally of the highest and, as a natural consequence, the return on funds, whether invested in securities or in commercial paper, is low by the individual's standards. For the other part of their business the banks may be looked upon as merchandisers of a commodity which is intangible but nevertheless extremely important in the modern business world. If credit is regarded as the commodity the banks have to sell, the interest rate received on loans stands as the equivalent of selling prices for an individual company.

2. *Long-term trends.* –In referring to trends in banking, we will consider only the banks of the large financial centers. Banks, being local institutions more so than are industrials, vary in policies and practices and generalization is difficult. But the central institutions have enough points in common to make generalization possible if the scope is confined to this class. Two changes in banking trends have taken place in the period since the end of World War I. Before the 1920's and, for a time, early in that decade, loans to business comprised the bulk of the banks' activities and investment was secondary. But about a third of the way though the decade a change appeared. Investments begat to take a larger place in the banks' earning assets. The importance of loans as earning assets declined. Nor has this condition shown evidence of changing back toward a restoration of the former relative importance of loans.

Another change is that which the decades of the 1920's and 1930's witnessed in the rise and the later elimination of investment-banking activities. The great output of securities in the decade following the end of the War found the large city banks participants, not directly but through the agency of affiliated companies which underwrote and distributed bond and stock issues. This was a source of earning power which had previously not appeared or, if experienced, had been of minor proportions, and the result of the sudden increment of large non-banking earnings was to make the bank stocks, along with securities in all other fields, active mediums of speculation.

This new source of income was short –lived, for the activity was curtailed by the banking legislation of recent years which required commercial banks to divest themselves of the affiliated companies by means of which investment-banking activities had been carried on.

The tendency toward increase in investments relative to loans has two effects on the position of banks regarded as investment mediums. The first tendency is toward reduction of earnings, for the rates obtainable on investments in prime short-term securities are normally considerably lower than the rates obtainable on loans to customers. A second effect is that, to whatever extent investment is directed to long-term rather than short-term issues, while a gain may have been made in liquidity as compared with a business loan, the gain has been at the cost of making the bank portfolio more responsive to major swings of the bond market.

In brief, a bank with a large part of its earnings assets in the form of loans encounters its chief hazard, in a period of declining business, in an increasing freezing or illiquidity of the loan items. One whose earning assets are primarily investments encounters its chief hazard in falling bond market which affects particularly the value of the long-term bonds in the portfolio.

3. *Deposits rise and fall with the business cycle.* –Banks have a threefold source of the raw materials lending and investing with which to work. The owned funds are represented by the bank's capital, surplus and undivided profits. A second source is that of a deposit, as when an individual or a corporation receives credit for the deposit of an assortment of cash and checks. This transaction, most aptly described as a primary deposit, adds to the earning assets of the bank in which the deposit is made but is obviously makes little change in the sum total of bank earning power, for the checks represent a transfer from one bank to another and the only new addition to the banking system's earning assets would be the cash items, or checks disbursing government funds.

In contradistinction to primary deposits are those which arise in the process of extending loans to customers. L when a loan is extended, represented by the customer's deposit, on the one hand, and his note in the bank's portfolio, on the other, an earning asset is created. Changes in the demand for credit, it is apparent, will normally exert more of an effect on the quantity of earning assets than changes proceeding from primary deposits, and since the demand for loans is normally active when business is brisk and sluggish when business is slack, the sum total of deposits tends to follow closely the swing of business cycle from prosperity to depression and back. In the latter half of the 1920's, deposits of the banks in principal cities increased sharply, reached a peak in 1928-1929, and then decline with the business depression. The low water mark for deposits was reached in 1933. Then with business recovery, they again expanded and by the end of 1936 they were at a new high level.

4. *Influence of money rates on earning power.* –If volume of deposits is a reflection of the volume of business which is being done, the rates obtainable on loans and investments stand, for the bank, in the place of selling prices of goods and services. A high volume of business done at rates which are low may be less remunerative than a smaller volume at high rates. For the purpose of illustration, the record of one bank through 1929 and the years following is presented. The selection is apt for the point, since earnings of this bank are not complicated by write-offs, and since its comparatively small volume of commercial business relative to its other activities makes the effect of changing money rates well reflected in the earnings.

In 1929, with deposits of $72,000,000 this bank showed earnings of $2,705,000 and the following year, with deposits of $58,000,000 earnings were over $4,000,000. In both of these years money rates were high and, after that 1929 panic, bond prices underwent a fair advance. Now, in each of the seven years following 1930, deposits were greater than the $58,000,000 of that year. By 1935 they were in excess of the 1929 total and by 1937 they were well over $80,000,000. But in only one year after 1930 were earnings as high as $2,000,000 and the showing of 1929 or of 1930 was not equaled, despite the materially larger volume of deposits. One important factor was the level of the money market, for in the years 1935-1937, when deposits were above the 1929 levels, rates on prime investments, particularly those of shore term were so low as to be, for the highest-grade and shortest-term issues, little more than nominal.

5. *Price movements of bank shares.* –The condition most favorable to high earning power is a combination of activity in the loan department of the banks' business coupled with a level of rates sufficiently high to make the volume of business remunerative. Since both volume and rates –particularly on investments –tend to fluctuate with changes in the business cycle, bank earning power and bank shares as investments are likewise subject to cyclical influence. In this connection, a general parallel between the course of bank stock prices and those of industrial stocks will be found to exist. In the period since the end of the war, industrials and bank shares rose in the two years after 1917, both reacted in the post-war bear market and both proceeded through the eight years following with their trends culminating in the rise which led to all-time highs in 1929, from which the descent was again parallel.

The influence of low money rates, of a comparatively restricted loan demand, and of the absence of investment-banking profits was witnessed, however, in the recovery after the bank holiday of 1933, for, whereas in the 1920's the courses of industrials and bank shares were closely parallel, with the latter performing at times more spectacularly than the industrials, the rate of improvement of bank stocks after 1933 was considerably slower than the rate of improvement of the industrials.

This, however, is not an unusual development but only a return to normal. It has been noted that the most elastic item of the banks' earning assets is the loan account. Now, a rising demand for loans comes from increased business activity. It is not something which precedes business activity. As a consequence, rises in bank profits tend to lag behind increases in industrial profits and the prices of bank shares tend to follow the general course of industrial stock prices rather than to lead.

In all normal cycles, then, bank shares should be considered along with industrials as hedges against changes in the purchasing power of money rather than as hedges against the fluctuations of business. The one condition which could operate to defeat this rule would be inflation so extreme as to react to an abnormal degree upon the dollar value of earning assets, for here, deposits being payable in dollars while the dollar value of investments was declining, the banks would obviously be squeezed.

6. *The capital structure of banks.* –Except in the cases of banks which have preferred stock, the capital structure of financial institutions would appear to call for no more than passing mention. And in the precise, technical meaning of the terms, a bank without preferred stock would properly be classed as one with a simple capital structure. As a practical matter, however, the very business of a bank is such as to make the earning power of its shares subject to the same kind of influence which operates on utilities, industrials or railroads, which have various relationships between owned and borrowed capital. To preserve the analogy, this natural banking set-up is treated as a problem of capital structure.

The similarity to any corporation with bonds outstanding lies in the fact that both bank and corporation are operating in part with owned capital, and in part with capital which is not owned. In the case of industrial or utility companies or railroads, the capital not owned is represented mainly by bonds; in the case of banks the outside funds are those of the bank's depositors. The corporation has a stable capital structure in that the outside funds are payable at a fixed time. The bank has a structure which is always in some flux since the outside funds are payable on demand.

The influence of the deposit total relative to capital funds on the earnings rate may be illustrated by the case of two banks, one of which, it will be supposed, does largely a commercial banking business while the other is more a specialist in trust and estate administration. The first bank has a capital of $2,000,000 and its surplus and undivided profits amount to $3,000,000 making $5,000,000 of the bank's owned funds which are at work. Deposits of this institution at the beginning of a year amount to $30,000,000 or six times the amount of the bank's owned funds. The second institution has a capital of $1,500,000 and surplus and undivided profits of the same amount, making $3,000,000 of owned funds, while its deposits total $9,000,000 or three times the amount of capital, surplus and undivided profits.

Now let us suppose that during the year the commercial bank earns at half the rate of the bank with the large trust business. Specifically, suppose the former to earn on its funds at the rate of ¾ of 1 per cent and the latter at the rate of 1 ½ per cent. Earnings of the former institution will then amount to $262,500 (¾ of 1 per cent on $35,000,000 the total of capital, surplus and undivided profits and deposits) while the second bank will earn $180,000 (1 ½ per cent on $12,0000,000 the total of its capital finds and deposits).

Set up in simple tabular form this data, and the results calculated from them to compare. Here the trust company has earned on its funds at double the rate of the commercial bank but on all owned funds the rate of earnings has been only ¾ of 1 per cent greater (6 per cent as compared with 5.25 per cent) while in terms of dollars per share of stock the commercial bank actually shows an advantage. In contrasted commercial enterprises where the depositors' funds are represented by funded debt, this result would be called the effect of leverage. The working of the rule is no less effective when the funds not owned are deposits or unfunded debt than when they are in the form of bonds or debentures.

Here the question is apropos as to what constitutes a fair ratio as between deposits and owned funds. To this there can be no categorical answer, for the relationship is one which will tend to vary in accordance with the business of banks or as between city and country banks, or as between banks in different sections, the last variation comprehending also differences as to type of business. The commercial bank in the foregoing illustration exhibits a ratio which would be perfectly normal for a large city institution doing a commercial business. The second bank's ratio of deposits to owned funds is unusually small, a fact which is the product in considerable measure of the nature of its business.

7. *Measurement of earning power.* –In comparing corporations whose businesses are at all alike, or in measuring the relative attractiveness of companies in different lines of business, the earnings per share of stock afford one simple basis of measurement. Earnings per share are computed for bank stocks and the figure is useful at least as a guide to cash dividend limitations. But the fact that banks normally have a large part of their owned funds represented by surplus and undivided profits makes the ratio of net income to the total of these items, or the capital funds, a more satisfactory measure of earning power and its trend.

8. *Valuation of bank shares.* –Bank stocks are still frequently valued on the basis of their record of earnings per share. If earnings per share are an imperfect measure of the bank's earning power, that are no less unsatisfactory, taken by themselves, as a gage of the value of a bank stock in the market.

A commonly used measure of value is one which differs sharply from the practice in valuing industrial, utility or railroads stocks. For issues in these groups book value is meaningless figure for any bearing it has on the market price of the stock. A chain-store stock with adequate earning power will regularly sell far above its book value, and a steel company, with its heavy capital investment, will regularly sell far below book value. But a bank differs from a commercial company. Its assets are loans and investments and, with the exception of is premises, it is able to transform its assets much more readily into cash. Book value measuring the earnings assets thus also becomes a measure of price, and by noting the relationships which customarily prevail in a given neighborhood between bank-share prices and book values, inferences may be drawn as to the value and attractiveness of these mediums of investment.

The ratio of price to book value will vary naturally with the state of the market. In times of speculative enthusiasm prices of leading bank shares have been quoted considerably above book values. Since the bottom of the post-1929 depression was reached there has been a tendency for prices to conform more nearly with book values than formerly. A group of seventeen New York banks, in the five years 1933-1937 inclusive, showed variations ranging from 2.20 times book values to 62 ½ per cent of book values for individual banks. At the highest prices of the five year period the stocks of the seventeen banks, averaged, sold at 1.52 times book values and at the lowest average prices they were quoted at 0.95 times book values. These ratios are under those which prevailed before 1929 and they suggest a norm of about 1 ¼ times book values, with fluctuations above and below that ratio in accordance with the general share market.

The average low ratios are of interest in another connection. Formerly the book value of bank shares was regarded as the cushion underneath the price. The quotation might rise above book value but it would never fall below it except briefly, and for trifling discounts then. But in the five-year period above, it will be noted that, at average low prices, the bank shares sold below book value, and, when individual cases are taken, the strength of the support accorded by this figure will appear less formidable. Of the seventeen banks, the shares of nine –a bare majority –averaged book value figures or over at the lowest price for the five-year period. But the prices of eight banks' shares when below book values at discounts ranging from 12 to as much as 46 per cent.

Advisory 7

Insurance Stocks

1. *Insurance stocks as investment media.* –Before the decade following
   WWI the average investor had little acquaintance with the stocks of
   insurance companies. As a matter of fact, the market was one which had
   to be sought out, for, being an over-the-counter market, the price
   movements of insurance company shares never assumed a prominent
   place, even in statistical tables, and little public attention was attracted to
   them either as investment or speculative media. A few over-the-counter
   firms specialized in bank and insurance shares and advertised their merits
   conservatively.

   But the speculative mania of the 1920's did not leave the insurance field
   untouched. Before the bull market had run its course insurance stocks
   were being widely urged upon investors and speculators. Their merits
   were extolled and, by the familiar method of comparing the growth of an
   invested dollar over a term of years, insurance shares appeared as one of
   the not limited number of roads to riches.

The depression which followed 1929 has served to prove the fallacy of the proposition that insurance shares, any more than other variety of stocks, move in the orbit of a perpetual bull market. In this revelation the investor is distinctly the gainer, for the approach to the investment proposition may be made in a matter-of-fact way and without the impression that the field is one devoid of risk. The market for insurance stocks is now probably wider than before the bull market of the 1920's, and the average investor is more likely to consider insurance shares for some place in his portfolio. The question is, what place? What advantages do insurance stocks offer and what particular role should they be expected to perform in any investment plan? In answering these questions, a brief consideration of the nature of the several kinds of insurance business, the sources of revenues, the possibilities of profit and of loss, and the risks to which insurance shares are peculiarly subject, are in order.

2. *Insurance companies.* –In size, whether measured by resources or by the annual volume of business, the life insurance companies are by far the most important division of the business. The great life insurance companies far exceed in size and in financial importance the largest units in other fields. But the nature of the life insurance business removes many of the most prominent companies from the investment field entirely. Such premier companies are owned by their policyholders –that is, they are mutual companies. The field of life insurance is not entirely removed from investment possibilities- some are stock companies- but it is a field in which the largest units are not the subjects of investment except as a policyholder may be considered an investor.

The most numerous group of companies whose shares are traded in on the over-the-counter market is the fire underwriters. The number of companies writing fire insurance is considerably more than those engaged in life insurance operations and, by contrast with the life underwriters, the fire insurance companies are mainly stock companies – corporations. A third group which is partially overlapped by the operations of some of the fire companies is made up of the casualty underwriters.

A fourth distinct group is composed of the companies which specialize in writing surety bonds or otherwise indemnifying against loss by default rather than loss through the hazard of fire or accident. For the purpose of completeness, marine insurance should be added, but this field is not important for the investment standpoint.

3. *Nature of the insurance operation.* –In all branches of insurance the work of the underwriter is that of indemnifying against a specific risk or risks. The nature of the risk differs with the field, and the nature of the risk accounts also for necessary differences in the method of operation of the companies. The writer of a policy of life insurance undertakes to indemnify on the happening of an event which is certain. There is no question as to the ultimate liability on any policy which is kept in force. The only question is when the liability will accrue.

The fact that the liability is certain and that only the time is uncertain makes it necessary for the life underwriter to purse an investment policy differing materially from that of the fire underwriter. The former's liability being to pay in dollars, his investments must be directed primarily to the maintenance of dollar values. The purchasing power of dollar is something which does not affect the life insurance company except as causes of variation in the purchasing power of money may affect the value of its investments. The obligation is to pay in dollars, and as long as the life insurance company follows an investment policy which assures it of an ample supply of dollars at all times for meeting accruing liabilities, its investment problem is met. The funds of these companies are, accordingly, invested mainly –or entirely –in securities which are promises to pay dollars, such as mortgages and public and corporate bonds. In many states the types of securities in which the funds of life insurance companies may be invested are prescribed by law and, in some, lists of securities which are legal for investment are promulgated by the state department having jurisdiction over the companies.

Turning from the life to the fire insurance companies, we find a difference at once apparent. The fire insurance company insures, not against a risk which is certain to happen, but against a risk which may never happen. Whereas the life insurance company must count upon meeting every policy which does not lapse, a fire insurance company may never incur any liability though it carry insurance upon a structure for centuries. This same line of division also marks off the casualty, surety and marine insurance companies from the life underwriter. The tornado may never occur; the bonded clerk may never default; the ship may never meet with a disaster at sea.

The fact that the liabilities of these companies are contingent rather than certain permits a greater latitude in investment policy. While any damage which is covered by a policy must be paid in dollars, it is certain that many policies will never call for payment. Hence the fire, casualty and other companies can invest, with perfect prudence, only part of their funds in securities which are promises to pay dollars –bonds and mortgages – and other parts of their funds may be employed, with perfect conservatism, in common stocks or other forms of investment which are shares of ownership rather than promises to pay.

Because of their greater number and importance in the investment field, the consideration of insurance companies as investments will be confined to the fire underwriters.

4. *Sources of income.* –To make clear the position of the insurance companies the sources of their income should be first considered. Their business is writing insurance against the risk of loss by fire or other contingency and their payment is the premium. Here is one source of income and one division of the business. But it is not the division which is ordinarily the most profitable. While the losses covered are contingent, every insurance company conducts its operations on an actuarial basis designed to make certain that the ability to meet extra-heavy as well as regular losses will not be wanting. As a consequence, the assets of such companies are large and fairly regular in proportion to their contingent liabilities to policyholders, and this fact makes the companies investors' year in and year out. The insurance company is, then, in part an underwriter and in part an investment trust and from the latter activity it derives its largest income.

5. *The unearned premium reserve.* –Another peculiarity of the fire insurance companies should be noted here in connection with their sources of income. The unearned premium reserve is not a separate source but it is a potential field for a deferred income which may become available at precisely the times when the business of industrial and commercial companies is at low ebb. When the policy is written the insurance company sets up the entire amount of the premium as a reserve. It is unearned and it will be earned only as the period covered by the policy runs. The reserve, moreover, is actually larger than the net amount received by the company, for whereas the whole premium is carried as unearned, the commission of the agent has actually been paid.

Now, as the policy runs through without loss the premium becomes earned. And it is clear from the nature of the operation that the larger the business done, the greater will be the funds of the company itself which are tied up in the unearned premium reserve. But, conversely, in a period when new writings decline, the decrease in the unearned premium reserve serves to swell profits apparently in the face of a declining volume.

6. *Underwriting ratios.* –A comparison of operation results in the form of ratios is of value for the information given, or the inference suggested, about various phases of the company's business. The comparison may be made vertically for the trend of results in the particular company under consideration, or it may be made horizontally –between two or more companies- for their relative performances or results, for one company may be compared with a general average for all companies for the purpose of seeing whether the individual record is above or below normal.

One ration bearing operation results is that of losses incurred to premiums earned. A rising trend of the ratio might suggest the need for greater strictness in the selection of risks, and this would be a natural inference if no other explanation of the trend were apparent. The period taken for comparison, however, must not be too short, or allowance must be made for the changes which take place in the state of business activity form year to year. A rising loss ratio for a short period of business depression might be attributable to the fact that the tendency to skimp on expenditures for maintenance in poor business years is a factor tending to increase combustion hazards.

If the first three years only were considered, a very marked rise would be apparent. But the period was one in which some increase in the loss ratio would be expected and consequently the short experience might be quite misleading as to efficiency. Taking the longer period, it is apparent that this company had an average ration of losses to premiums earned of 43.73 per cent. Comparing this recode with that of a score of other companies for the same period, we find only two with lower ratios, while the average for the twenty was over 47 per cent. On the comparison the longer trend, the showing of the company is better than average and, as the record shows, with the exception of two years, the ratio has been fairly constant.

The matter of interest here is the decline in the expanse ratio during the latest two years. Comparison with other companies shows the ratio to be higher than average, both for the period and for the latest year. This ratio is best considered, however, in connection with the trend of the volume of business, and it is related to the loss ration just considered.

The unearned premium preserve, as mentioned above, is set up for the entire amount of premiums written. But the agent's commission is payable at once and thus a rising volume of insurance effected may have a tendency to raise the expense ratio. Its connection with the loss ratio is through the factor of risk selection. Obviously if a thorough and careful investigation of risks is made, the cost of obtaining business will be higher than if a more casual policy is followed. But the extra care and expense may well be rewarded by a lower than average loss ratio. As a consequence, in the case which has been under consideration here, having found a loss ration materially lower than the average and a ratio of expenses to premiums which is higher than average, we would conclude that extra care and expense in writing business was being compensated for by a lower rate of losses paid.

The combination of losses incurred and the expense of underwriting, deducted from the amount of earned premiums, gives the underwriting gain of the company. For the latest year of the period which has been considered, the subject company reported premiums earned of $11,236,000; its underwriting expense amounted to $5,905,000, and it paid losses amounting to $4,799,000. The net underwriting gain for the year was $559,000 and this was nearly 5 per cent -4.69 per cent- of the earned premiums. For the year in question this ratio was slightly below average. Over a term of years the ratio may rise as high as 10 per cent for some companies, or fall to 2 or 3 per cent. A showing of between 5 to 7 per cent may be taken as a fair average performance under average conditions, although this should not be taken as a hard-and-fast rule. Comparisons should be a made with a representative group of companies for actual trends and results, as the illustrations of other ratios set out above.

7. *Investment operations.* –The importance of the investment operations of a fire insurance company may be illustrated by carrying the underwriting profit of the company under consideration of a few steps further. It has been noted that during the latest year the company earned $559,000. Underwriting profit and loss charges reduced this amount to $548,000,

which stands as the final net result of underwriting operations. During the year the income of the company from interest and rentals amounted to $1,125,000 which is more than double the net gain from underwriting. Other investment gains, net, brought the total to $1,159,000 so that the combined gain from underwriting and investment activities amounted to $1,707,000, of which underwriting accounted for 32.1 per cent and investment operations for 67.9 per cent. This result is not exceptional. It is, on the contrary, in line with the regular operations of the fire insurance companies, which, as has been indicated, are part underwriters of risk and part investment trusts.

8. *The investment portfolio.* –The description of fire insurance companies as part investment trusts is accurate, for not only do they regularly derive a large proportion of income from their investment operations, but the latter, being flexible, are capable of being handled in much the same manner as the funds of a management investment trust. It has been noted that the line of differentiation between the investment policies of life and fire insurance company is that laid down by the nature of the risk. Since the risk assumed by the fire insurance company is one which may happen, but which is not certain to happen, it is not under the compulsion of having its assets in the form of securities which are promises to pay dollars.

It can, and does, hedge against the dollar risk in its investments. Portfolios will be found well divided at any one time as among bonds, mortgages and preferred stocks, on the one hand, and equities represented by stocks, on the one hand, and equities represented by stock of the other insurance companies and other equities, on the other. The proportion of holdings in each group will be found to vary also from period to period in accordance with the company's judgment of the relative weight of these risks.

A comparison of the distribution of representative companies' portfolios at two periods, widely differing in the prevailing state of business activity, in the condition of the securities markets, and in the supply of loan able funds, will illustrate at once the distribution of portfolios and the policies of managements. The year 1932 closed with the shadow of depression deep and with the banking situation so strained that, within less than ten weeks, all banks in the country were to be closed. The companies included held various proportions of common stocks, but the insurance stock holdings and other common stocks, but the insurance stock holdings and other common stocks together bulked large in the portfolios.

A company had more than half of their investments in equities –insurance and common stocks. The great majority held over a third of their funds in stocks. Bearing on individual policies, it is of interest to note the entire absence of real estate loans from the portfolios. Investment policies were at the bottom of a bear market. Now with but minor interruptions, common stocks underwent an advance for the next four years. At the end of 1936 prices were practically at the top of a long bull market. The bear market, which ran through 1937, was unfavorable for investments in equities and, to a less marked extent to investment in any type of security except bonds of the highest grade and of short-term maturity.

A comparison of a general increase in cash and its equivalent, with prices high, compared with the position four years previously. Another change at once apparent is the general decrease in the proportion of real estate loans. As against the smaller loans on realty, holdings of insurance stocks show a general gain. The investment in common stocks other than insurance companies was reduced.

9. *The balance sheet.* –For the railroad, public utility or industrial, the book value or equity of the stock is unimportant for any bearing it has on market price. But in the case of insurance companies, book value is a figure which may be transformed into liquidating value without too great a disparity between the apparent equity and the figure which may be realized. This fact proceeds, of course, from the nature of the assets. Fixed assets or current assents in the form of inventories, supplies, finished goods or fixtures can be sold at only a small percentage of their values as carried on the average balance sheet, if liquidation is forced. But the insurance companies' investments are largely in marketable securities or in investments which, if not possessing a free market, are nevertheless capable of appraisal and purchase as investments by others.

On the liability side of the balance sheet, the major items are the capital of the company, its surplus, the unearned premium reserve, and losses payable. The first three of these items represent the shareholders' equity and the capital and surplus may be taken together. The unearned premium reserve, however, is not all equity for the stockholders. Part of it is for, as has been noted, this reserve is the full premiums which have been paid in and which are transformed form unearned to earned with a passage of the terms of the individual insurances that comprise the whole of the company's underwriting. In calculating the equity of shareholders in the reserve, the establishment rule is to take 40 per cent of the figure. While matters might work out with a variation from this standard in any actual liquidations, the ration is based on experience, and using the one percentage as a standard gives a uniform method for appraising the liquidating value of all companies.

Say, now, we have a company with a capital of $9,398,000, represented by 1,880,000 shares, and that it has a surplus of $11,073,000 and an unearned premium reserve of $12,277,000. The total value of the shareholders' equity is $9,938,000, plus $11,073,000, plus 40 per cent of $12,277,000 or $4,911,000. These three items total $25,382,000 and this divided by the number of shares, gives a value of $13.50 for the stock. Some changes may be rung on the calculation where there are ascertainable differences between the value of the assets as carried on the books and their market values.

10. *Valuation of insurance stocks.*-The difference just indicated between the importance of book value in the case of insurance companies and industrials rails and utilities is not without its bearing on methods of valuing the stocks as investments. As with companies in other lines, it is possible to work out ratios between prices and earnings which may be useful as a general guide. But the importance of investment income and of appreciation, both realized and unrealized, in the insurance company's earning; power, and the direct bearing of these operations on the shareholder's equity, gives a simpler yardstick in the relationship between the equity per share and the market price.

It must be understood that this, like any other investment ratio, is not something static. It is subject to change in accordance with changes in the level of business activity, the earning power of money and the profitableness, or otherwise, of the insurance companies' operations. Nor will ratios be the same naturally, in bull and bear markets. But with the necessity for periodical revision understood, data may be derived which will serve as a general and reasonably accurate yardstick for measuring the attractiveness of a representative stock as an investment.

Bearing on the matter of changing ratios, it may be noted that there has been a tendency for a less optimistic valuation to be placed on the insurance companies as investment mediums than was the case in the heyday of their popularity. A ratio of from 1 ½ to 1 ¾ times the equity was at one time regarded as a not over sanguine rule of valuation. But in the years which followed 1929 a revision in the market valuation appeared. Taking a group of ten leading companies for the years 1930 to 1936, inclusive, at the best prices for which they were quoted on the average, the market would have shown a figure of no more than 1.4 times the equity per share. AT the opposite extreme, taking the lowest average prices for this period, the shares were quoted at 80 per cent of the equity per share.

These ratios would have stood for indications of the upper and lower limits of valuation in 1937. In brief, a stock which was then found selling at above 1.4 times the equity must have been regarded as at least very fully priced, on the record, and presumably as selling somewhat too high –and the consideration of this fact must have lead to an avoidance of the shares prices were quoted at above the higher ratios, and a selection either of issues in the group more reasonably valued, if satisfactory stocks could be found, or else of issues from some other field altogether. This latter alternative leads directly to the question of the place of insurance company stocks in an investment portfolio.

11. *Insurance stocks as investments.* –By far the greater number of insurance stocks are traded in over the counter –that is, they are not listed on exchanges. For the shares of leading companies, however, an active market is maintained and quotations of bid and asked prices are available. In the broad, general grouping, insurance stocks are to be classed with those securities whose place in the investment portfolio is to hedge against fluctuations in dollar purchasing power. They tend to move with the general market, as is entirely natural because of their investment operations. The leverage factor which has been mentioned and the quality of management, as well as the distribution of investments, suggests three uses for insurance company shares in an investment plan.

Taking these factors up in reverse order, it is clear that insurance company stocks offer an excellent means of diversifying for the investor whose funds or not large enough to permit his attaining much diversity himself. The purchase of the stock of one insurance company by an investor with a few thousand dollars, for instance, spreads his funds over a greater number of stocks than he could possibly obtain in any reasonably sized lots by his own direct investment.

The second utility of these stocks is linked with this diversity, for if an investor has neither the time nor the experience to attend actively to his own affairs nor funds large enough to employ counsel, the insurance stocks act as an automatic retainer of a skilled management. This statement is not to advance the proposition that investments should not be watched, for the nature of the insurance companies' primary business imposes natural limitations upon freedom of action. In a time when funds ought to be largely liquid, the individual investor is more free to cash in on his investments than the institutional investor. But for the classes and for the purposes suggested these shares have a definite place.

Insurance stocks have a place in larger portfolios particularly at the beginning of long cyclical upswings in the market. The leverage factor is the reason for such investment. When the tide begins to run toward higher prices, insurance company shares are in a position to hold their own with the market and to keep pace with its advances.

Advisory 8

Investment Trusts.

1. *Purpose of investment trusts.* –The term "investment trust" is used here as being the familiar designation of a group of companies, although the trust form of organization is not used by any of the companies whose issues are at all well known and "Investment Company" or "Corporation" describes the enterprise better. Whatever its type, an investment trust functions principally as a means for gathering together the funds of individual investors through sale to them of its own securities and investing these funds in the securities of the industrials, railroads, public utilities, bands, or other enterprises and, possibly participation in the underwriting of the securities of some of these organizations. It is, to carry precision in definition a step further, actually a reinvestment company, for two investment operations are a necessary feature of its operation –the primary investment of individual shareholders or bondholders in the securities of the investment trust and the reinvestment of these funds by the latter in standard listed securities.

   Investment trusts have functioned in the London market for many decades. Their growth in North America was slow and reached important proportions only in the decade following the War. But once the growth was started, it assumed mushroom dimensions and characteristics.

A more truly indicative description of certain of the enterprises and some of the practices of the trusts of pre 1929 days would have been "speculative trusts." The difficult years since the days when market profits were easy of attainment have served to restore the investment trust to the position it should rightfully occupy and, while stripping it of the glamour of a vehicle for profit, have emphasized its rightful place and have shown its ability to function, and to function reasonably well under adverse conditions.

2. *Types of investment trusts.*-A number of classifications of investment trust might be made. They may be graded as to the elasticity or rigidity of their management, as to their character, whether mutual or otherwise, or as the general or limited field of investment within which they operate. All types can be comprehended in a survey of the field, form trusts of elastic to those of rigid management.

The first group would comprise all trusts in which the management has an unlimited discretion in the investment of funds of the company, as to security, as to time of purchase and as to time of sale. Trusts of this kind are essentially of the English pattern with variations in practice and operation. Within this general management group of trusts, however, a number of different plans and corporate set-ups are to be found.

A mutual trust is one which must maintain a market for its own shares, buying them from investors at a price which conforms to the shifting value of the portfolio. The market price of a mutual investment trust stock, accordingly, will conform at all times to the going value of the company as that value is reflected in the shareholder's pro-rata interest in it. The mutual company is required to distribute not less than 90 per cent of its earnings in dividends to its shareholders, its right to create funded debt is limited, and it is further restricted as to the extent of its investment in individual securities or in individual companies.

A management investment trust which is not a mutual, is an investing corporation. Its share may, or may not, be listed on an exchange and, since the corporations not bound to purchase its own securities, their value may deviate from the indicated worth of the shares as shown by the investment trust's balance sheet. These deviations follow the tone of the stock market – in a bull market shares of investment trusts have sold at prices considerably above their indicated worth if the company should be forthwith dissolved, while the depression markets the same shares have sold at figures considerably less than would be required to duplicate the portfolio which they represent.

Shares of such management companies, in effect may represent virtually, although not legally, a direct pro-rata interest in the portfolio if the corporations has no bonds or preferred stock outstanding. An example of a trust on the New York Stock Exchange the shares may be junior to a preferred issue, or they may be deferred to the prior claims of both creditors and senior stockholders.

These are differences in form and organization, but, whatever the corporate structure, if no restrictions are imposed upon the management, the company is a management trust.

3. *Limited management trust.* –The discretion of a management may be circumscribed by various provisions. It may be limited, for instance, as to the proportion of funds which may be invested in the securities of one company, or in one security, or the field of investment may be narrowed to a stated list of securities. Here while the management has full secretion as to the division of funds within the approved list, it may not invest outside the list, no matter how attractive the security.

Trusts organized under the limited form stand in a position midway between the management trusts where full discretion is permitted and the rigid type where there is a minimum of management control over the portfolio.

4. *Unit trusts.* –Investment trusts of the rigid form are known as fixed or unit-type trusts. Either term is descriptive because a group of securities is selected and funds are invested strictly within the given list, with provision usually made for some substitution or change under stated conditions. The list may be comprehensive, attempting a cross-section of the whole market, or it may be specialized as to industry. Thus Company A, covered a large number of representative companies. By contrast, the several individual units of Company A offer portfolios composed entirely of railroad-equipment shares, petroleum shares, or shares in a number of other special fields.

5. *Growth of investment principles.* –While the principles of management and unit-type trust organization and administration have undergone but little change, it has required some practical demonstration of the desirable and undesirable to crystallize these principles. In the fixed-trust field, as far as the portfolio composition was concerned, the most unsound practice among the early trusts was the provision for elimination of a stock which passed its dividend. Where the requirement was absolute, this provision menat, in effect, that the trust, to that extent, was bound to follow the highly unsound practice of selling out individual parts of its portfolio at bottom prices. A restriction which would compel a sale at a high price would be sound. One forcing sale at a low price would mean a forced dissipation of capital.

Among the management trusts, a principle of general application is that investment income, by which is meant interest and dividends as distinguished from market profits, ought to be sufficient to cover fixed charges and preferred dividends. The reason for this requirement is clear. Interest charges must be met if the corporation is to keep

going. Preferred dividends ought to be met, for if an investment company cannot handle its funds so as to meet a payment which is certain and calculable, doubts must arise as to the efficacy of its management. The only way to be certain of meeting these charges is to have the portfolio so invested that there is a certain income to balance against the certain outgo. Of course, how exact the balance needs to be may vary in accordance with the financial status of different trusts. Company
a for example, failed to earn its full preferred dividend for the years 1932-1935 inclusive, but the distribution was paid without interruption.

6. *Flexibility and rigidity in theory and practice.* –The central theory back of the management investment trust is that an experienced and capable directorate and management ought to be able to invest funds better, and to manage them better, than the average inexperienced investor. The trust's principal service is making an expert management available to the general public. Since the integrity of the management is not likely to be called into question-there is no point to hedging its discretion with rules and limitations.

At the opposite pole from the management trust is the unit-type trust which, in principle, tires to remove management, with its inevitable errors of judgment, as a factor and places its reliance on the assumed normal growth of business over the long term. The assumption is that unless the country's economic life passes into a positive retrogression, business will grow from one period to another, corporations will share in the growth, and a selection of leading companies will float, so to speak with the times. Normal growth is considered a more reliable vehicle of success than expertness in management.

In a midway position, the limited management type resembles the flexible in giving a more prominent place to active management but in setting up limitations on the exercise of discretion, usually with regard to the choice of securities.

There are some points in favor of, and against, each of the several arrangements. The most logical form of the trust is the flexible management type. If an investor is going to invest at second hand –that is through the intervention of another party- the most practical method is the selection of the most capable management which can be found and then giving that management full rein. In support of this position, it may be argued that it is no more logical to provide a presumably expert management for funds and then to limit the activities of the management than it is to give careful thought to the selection of a lawyer or an architect and then to limit the professional man's sphere of activity.

An argument for setting up the unit-type trust may be that managements have proved themselves to be far from perfect and that, in some instances, performance has actually been worse than random selection. Hence the investor is better off if he gets altogether rid of the human factor, with its fallible judgment. The conclusion, however, rests upon three assumptions which cannot be taken for granted. First, the assumption that the long-term course of business must inevitably be upward rests upon the history of a developing nation. Will the same thing be true of a nation which has reached economic maturity? Second, although provisions have been made against human error in management, the original selection of securities is a matter of judgment, and fallibility may be manifest in the initial choice as well as in the later handling of a portfolio.

Finally, the one sure rule of life is that nothing is certain as change. Economic history is studded with the record of industries which have flourished and waned; of companies which have enjoyed a decade or more of prosperity and then either failed or entered a period when their fortunes appeared definitely a period when their fortunes appeared definitely to fade; or events arising in domestic politics or in international affairs which have abruptly changed the course of economic events. The vehicle which is best adapted to meet sudden change is primarily better equipped to make headway than the one which is committed to a program, or to investment in specific industries or companies which may later prove to be far from the best selections from the entire investment field.

7. *The investment trust as a profit vehicle.* –Particularly in the formative stage, the pre 1929 period, the major emphasis was laid upon the profit-making possibilities of expert management. That point still likely to be stressed. But on the point records are more apropos than words. The following summary traces the record of three trusts for the period 1929 to 1936 and, it must be emphasized, the record is not presented as a derogatory reference either to management trusts as a group, or to the three trusts selected individually. On the contrary, the three trusts have been chosen for the express reason that their sponsorship was excellent and their managements were regarded as among the most content. Measured by the net assets per share applicable to the stocks, the records from 1929 to 1936.

The year 1929 was followed by three years of falling prices for securities, and these in turn by two years of moderate and two of brisk recovery. While the tide was adverse the value of shares in all the trusts declined, and when the tide was favorable good progress was made.

The record may readily be better than that which an individual could make handling his own funds, but an investment medium which must place its funds in securities influenced by the swings or the business cycle cannot be immune to the ups and downs of that cycle. The investment trust is a medium for profits when conditions are favorable. When they are adverse, it is no more likely to make money than the individual. It is reasonably likely, however, to lose ground at a lesser rate than the general market.

Two different trusts can change the proportion of their investments as between equities, fixed-income securities, and cash or its equivalent, form year to year.

A study of representative investment trusts for the period 1930-1936, inclusive, showed a rate of decline 5 ½ per cent less than that of the general market, but a rate of increase in the recovery of the subsequent three years about 25 per cent less than the rate for the market. As a result, the net decrease for the trusts in the six-year period was at a rate between four and five per cent greater than that of the general market. Again, in the declining market of 1937, a group of representative trusts lost ground at a rate 4 ½ per cent greater than a standard average of industrial shares.

8. *Place of the investment trust.* –While some free outstanding exceptions may be found, it is clear from the record that, on the experience thus far available, the investment trust is not a vehicle adapted to profit making. Nor is the reason obscure. Unless a trust is sufficiently sure of its position to go practically 100 per cent into common stocks in the early stages of a bull market when percentage appreciation is greatest, its investments are very likely to be less satisfactory than a reasonably well selected group of stocks. And since depreciation in a bear market is apparently something which can only be cushioned rather than avoided, the lower gain in an investment trust in a bull market, together with the loss-even though less than the average –in a bear market, is not an inviting combination.

But to make this statement is not to say that the management trusts have not a place in the investment field. They perform one useful and valuable service in that they are a vehicle by which the investor with limited means can obtain a degree of diversification which would otherwise be impossible. Even in tenshare lots the diversification of $500, $1,000 or $2,000 cannot be very satisfactory unless low-priced stocks exclusively are selected. But the amount invested in a well-managed trust, while at the hazard of the market, is less at the hazard of single industries.

If the case for the management trusts thus narrows to their value as a diversification medium, still less can be said in favor of the fixed trust. The purchaser of the usual fixed trust is paying a healthy premium for his diversification and, moreover, in the case of sale, the spread between bid and asked prices makes an appreciable difference in the value of his funds invested and their value converted into cash.

A paradoxical situation is presented both by the management and fixed trusts in this matter of diversification, which is their strongest claim to investment favor. In proportion as diversification increases –i.e., the more widely the fund is spread –the closer the fund comes to resemble the general market and the more likely is its performance to be that of a market as a whole. Now, if the greater the diversification the more likely is the performance to parallel that of the general market, it follows that the greater the utility of the trust as a vehicle for spreading the risk the less adapted it is to showing capital gains better than the market itself over a term of years.

9. *Installment funds.* –A comparatively new outgrowth of the investment trust movement is the existence of trusts or funds which pool the investments of participants, not through sale of shares outright but by their sale on an installment plan, so that the investor pays small amounts regularly for a period of years, receiving the addition of earnings on his participation to accelerate the rate of growth of his interest. The plan, in method and in time, finds a general likeness in installment savings-and-loan association shares.

Again, plans of this sort have a function to perform but it is essential that the exact nature of that function be understood by the investor or prospective investor. If a person wishes to lay aside a fixed amount each month and he already has a fair backlog of savings accounts, bonds or mortgages –all forms of investment sited to preserve dollars –a medium which permits periodical investment in a group of stocks helps balance his risk. If, however, an investor or prospective investor has no backlog of cash, bonds or other investments to conserve dollars, he ought not to enter into the accumulation of any sums in any vehicle which has as its nucleus common stocks, under the impression that he is saving in the ordinary acceptation of that term. He is putting away dollars but what he will receive in the way of dollars ultimately is uncertain.

The sales talk will be that the country is bound to grow, industry is bound to grow and fabulous profits accrue to those who take a long-term position on the growth of industry. The obverse side is that industry occasionally goes down-hill as well as up-hill; that the nearer to economic maturity a country is, the less probable it is that spectacular profits are likely to feature generally rising trends of the business cycle' that an investor who started putting away money regularly in 1920 to buy common stocks, kept up the process for 10 or 11 years, and received a certificate in 1931, would probably have been in an unhappy frame of mind.

The test of plans of this general nature for adaptability to an investment program is the same as for any security –does it promise to pay dollars at a future date and in a certain amount? If so it is an instrument for saving dollars. If it does not explicitly promise to pay dollars but if the value depends upon market prices, the device is not adapted for saving at all but it is adapted to hedging against the possibility of a rise in the cost of living. IT possesses elements of possible gain and the risk of possible loss, which are the inevitable complement of all investment forms which are hedges against rises in living costs.

10. *Profit opportunities in investment trusts.* –The price of shares of a mutual investment trusts and the asset value of the shares will always correspond, for, since the shares are convertible into the assets of the fund or their cash equivalent, they cannot sell below break-up value nor would any informed investor pay more than this figure for them. For example, a mutual trust has a net asset value of $15.25 per share. No stockholder will sell at less than this figure, for he can obtain that amount from the trust itself. Nor would a buyer offer more, since his only assured market is the asset or conversion value. The prices of investment trusts which are not mutuals, however, have held varying relationships to asset values, according to the state of the market and the subjective valuation which investors place upon securities.

In the days of investment-trust craze, previous to the 1929 panic, many management trusts, particularly those with bonds or preferred stocks outstanding, sold for multiples of the break-up values. The jargon of the day labeled this a "premium on management." It was actually irrational speculation pushed to its limit, for, if a trust is trading on the equity to the extent of having fixed-income securities ahead of its own common, its shares are among the most vulnerable of securities in a falling market. If asset value is paid for its shares, there is the assumption of a high degree of risk, but paying more than asset value for a leverage trust is equivalent to making a voluntary offer to lay odds of 3 to 1 when the bookmaker is offering 4 to 1.

The reverse of this situation occurred in the depression market of the years after 1929. A trust such as Fourth National Investors, with no bonds or preferred stock outstanding, habits shares quoted in the market at less than the net asset value –and the portfolio of the trust was high grade. This was an opportunity, such as is seldom given, of acquiring representative stocks, listed on the New York Stock Exchange, at substantial discounts from the prevailing market prices.

Situations such as this present an almost certain profit opportunity for discerning investors. In the long run, the judgment of the market on values will be found accurate, but that judgment is subject to many aberrations. If at any time an investment trust which has no bonds, preferred stocks, bank loans, or other claims or preferences ahead of the common shares, is discovered with those shares selling well below indicated asset values, the investor has about as certain an opportunity for profit as he will find in the market. At the worst, if values continue to decline, the fall in the price of the stock, already inordinately low, should be slower than the drop in the market and in the net asset value of the shares. On the favorable side, in any market when the judgment or the nerve of investors is better, the price may be expected to conform to asset value. If it does no more than this there is a small profit, Better still, if the conformation is achieved while prices are rising, there is a two-fold source of profit –in the rise of the general market, lifting asset values, and the faster rise of the market, lifting asset values, and the faster rise of the price of the trust shares as the discount is obliterated.

11. *Diversification of trusts.* –Just as diversification is carried to illogical extremes in individual lists, so investors sometimes look for profit or safety by spreading a fund over a number of investment trusts. This is not only carrying diversification to a point beyond the limit of sound policy but it is also a procedure likely to defeat the purpose, if the purpose is profit, by bringing about, in part, the fruitless result which would follow if one were to buy and simultaneously sell the same amount. A fund is spread between trusts; as a result the policy of one trust is partially negative by the policies of the others.

A diversified investment-trust list, as distinguished from a diversified industrial, utility and railroad list, is one which exposes the fund to managements working at cross purposes. One investment trust will give the average investor all the diversification he needs and it will give a unified management. It is likely to be better than several managements. The remedy, if the investment proves less satisfactory, apparently, than others, is to change managements.

Advisory 9

Selling Stock Profit from Declining Stocks

The popular purpose to invest in stock is with the anticipation and hope that the stock will rise in value. Everybody is aware that there are corrections in the market and the stock goes down at times. Selling short is simply a bet where you can make money when the market is going down. You will find the details explained with the following explanation. If you are a good predictor of the economy and trends in the market, money can be made. However, this may be a bit more gambling than a conservative investor wishes to engage in.

Most people are under the impression that stock market profits are derived from stocks increasing in value.

This report will give a view of profits that can be attained from declined stock prices.

"Long" and "Short" <u>Buying</u> and Selling

When you buy a security you go "long" on the stock. When you sell stock which you haven't previously bought you are "selling short," which means that you will later have to buy the stock in order to deliver it to whoever bought it from you. You buy "long" when you believe a stock will advance, and you "sell short" when you believe that it will fall in value. Thus, if you sell a stock short at 135 today, and tomorrows, or later, the price goes down to 133, you buy "to cover" your sale, you profited two points.

The average person buying and selling stock does not often sell short. It is human nature and habit to go forward, to be optimistic, just as a person rarely walks backward. However, the same opportunities in selling long are available to those who sell short. Some cynics say the public is the "bull" (for selling "long") while the inside operators are those who usually are "bears" who "sell short"). The only truth in this is the known fact that the public usually stays out of a falling market. It is afraid of it, for rather simple-minded reasons. But selling short is quite logically a part of the technique of the stock market. The "shorts" or "bears" are foils to the excessive optimism of the "longs," or "bulls," who might otherwise push market prices up out of all reason.

And, since stocks must move both up and down, as any chart of stock prices shows there is every reason why stock traders should not sell both "long" and "short."

A necessary element in successful trading on the side, is an ability to turn the processes of one's mind backwards as readily as forward; to analyze with the same accuracy and facility the factors which send values downward, as one analyzes the factors making for the upward course of values. This for some people is rather tempermentally impossible.

There are two types of "short selling," as there are two types of "long selling"--the trading for quick turns, and the trading for "long pulls," or periods of a month or a year or more.

Sometimes there is discussed the "unsound ethics" of short selling--"selling what you haven't got"--but this is an exploded idea. "Contracts to sell, to deliver in the future property not possessed at the time, is common to ordinary business; and legally is the well settled common law of the country."

Short selling takes place in every line of business. The farmer needing money in the spring, after sowing wheat or planting cotton, goes to a merchant or to a bank and sells his anticipated crop at a named price, to be delivered in October. If the crop does not equal the amount sold the farmer must buy enough to make a full delivery according to the terms of the sale. If the price he pays is less than the prices at which he sold in the spring, then he makes a profit on the purchase; if more, then he takes a loss.

A majority of traders and speculators favor the buying side of the Stock Market, a minority the selling or short side. The more experience one has in trading, the more one is inclined to operate on both sides, thus taking advantage of movements in either direction.

In selling short one must always buy in ("cover") that which is sold short, since no delivery can be made until this is done.
The transaction is not completed until the purchase is made and the stock delivered. The broker, however, may and usually does borrow the amount of stock sold short and deliver it for the short seller, thus deferring an actual purchase to cover. So a short sale may run for an indefinite period--weeks, days, months--but ultimately the stock must be bought and delivered before the trader can take his profit, just as long stock must be sold before the profit is realized.

An interesting advantage in short selling is this--there are no interest charges on a short sale.

Taking a "Bull" or "Bear" Position

This first necessity in stock trading is to determine the
fundamental position to take in the market, to buy or to sell; to determine that values will go higher or go lower.

Next, will they go lower or higher, or ?

Naturally, to arrive at an opinion on the fundamental position of the market is the more complicated, the more difficult--and also the more vitally important in any general trading. Like a mariner who sails west when he wants to go east, a man making a hasty decision would soon come to grief. Data on fundamental conditions for a month, for six months, for a

75

year, for two, three or four years are necessary. Almost every type of knowledge and fact has a bearing on the situation: politics, industry, economics, world happenings--even psychology.

If the average of prices and another factors during the period of time show an ascending scale, indicating the tide rising a little higher in each successive wave, then one is justified in concluding the market is a Bull Market at some stage of development or completion. Securities should then be bought on sharp recessions. If, on the other hand, the average of prices running back over a like period, show each wave reacting lower than the preceding one, and the rallies or rebounds fall short of the former ones, then one may be justified in concluding it is a Bear Market, starting or reaching middle or end and one should sell securities.

Thus, the trader places himself intelligently in the general scheme, like the sea captain who "takes his position" from the heavens. Of course the subject at the moment is always controversial; there are always two opinions. One must decide for himself his own opinion which then establishes a direction. That is what makes the market.

Such a bull or bear position is divisible into a classification by length. Thus, there may be two-year bears, who believe that prices must fall for the next two years; there may be one-year bears. six-month bears and three month or month bears. There are recession bears; who merely look for breaks lasting from one hour to a week or two. Conversely, the same is true of bulls. "What goes up must come down" is an old Wall Street adage, comforting to bears.

"Panics" and depressions, are according to Federal Reserve Bank charts, showing less and less frequency and also—more important perhaps---less and less range of fluctuation. This indicates better business management, a better monetary system and greater intelligence in watching fundamental indicators.

Chart systems and basic trend lines are often as dangerous as they may be useful, because of error and dogmatic assumptions. The cycle theory has proved rather chimerical, as the periodicity of panics and inflation has not occurred according to prediction. The failure to predict fundamentals is one of the outstanding facts of Wall Street.

Hindsight and Foresight

In 1914, just before the Great War broke out in Europe, the market was under severe pressure and had become so dull·and listless that many brokers were giving up business. When war was actually declared by the various foreign governments the market went into a spasmodic break in which values played no part. Stocks were thrown over right and left and it was necessary to close the Exchange for several months until the foreign financial outlook could assume an even keel.

The wild Bull Market that followed in 1915 and 1916 is common history. During this period shrewd investors in Wall Street made far more quick money than had ever been made before in an equal time. The steel, automobile and rubber stocks were the leaders and went to unheard of heights, considering their value a few years previous. The depression that carried out the early theory that an orgy of speculation on one side of the market is always followed by the same result on the other side.

The market climbed to still greater heights in 1919 and it reflected illusions of the day which were soon transmitted to prices for commodities, on the whole community's belief that a shortage of everything existed as a consequence of the war, and that no limit could be assigned to the purchase of home and foreign consumers. When it suddenly became plain, first, that the movement both in commodities and on the Stock Exchange had been based upon excessive and unwarranted use of credit (which had obviously greatly overstrained the banks), and, second, that the foreign buying power had been as grossly overestimated as the home supply of goods had been underestimated, the end came with disastrous violence. We then had to face the famous deflation period.

The 1925 Bull Market was the longest on record and was not accurately forecast, and had in it some very difficult factors to analyze. All of which illustrates the great importance of determining as clearly as may be possible the fundamental position of the market. There are at least 25 different factors which have weight in any analysis and most of them are available in statistical reviews and reporting services.

More recently the "Crash of '87" represented one of the greatest profit opportunities in history. A single short S&P 500 future positions could have delivered an amazing $60,000--without even picking a top or bottom. However, we have the benefit of 20/20 hindsight. Could we have spotted the Crash in time to profit?
If so, could we have maintained the cool discipline required to stay with short positions long enough to take advantage of "Black Monday" and moves that followed?

The answer to the first question is obviously yes. It is the second question so many must answer in the negative. In reality, few were able to sustain positions through the wild swings that took place the week before Black Monday.

An examination of the December S & P 500 chart reveals that the market held support at 3100 throughout October 12. This area was tested in mid-September and late August. In addition, the June/July consolidation held above 3100 for more than four weeks. Therefore, strict chartists should have sold the S & P 500 on October 12, 13 or 14. The support was violated. Furthermore, the 10-day moving averages had been penetrated.

The fundamentals also supported a strong stock market correction. Federal Reserve Board managed to shrink the value of T-bounds by more than 15 percent, T-notes by nearly 10 percent, T-bills by equivalent amounts. The result of this massive nonliquidity was to force institutions to "cash in" their stocks to regain lost principal values. This action was solely responsible for the Crash.

Fundamentals Analysis

Huge budgets and trade deficits are only an excuse for poor judgement. While there is no doubt that contributed to government debt conditions prior borrowing, were the same as they were after. The only difference was the crash, where severe constraint placed on the money supply by raising interest rates.

Given the clear signals to go short on equities and government instruments, we might assume that all technical traders made a killing. Yet, the reality is that many technicaltraders were killed. Memories fade fast. However, anyone trading on October 12 will recall that just after 3100 was penetrated, the market rallied sharply. The following day, prices broke through 3150 on the upside. To many, this was a reversal of the technical sell signal.

Popular forecasters called for the Dow Jones Industrial Average to "correct" to 2300. They strongly recommended buying equities once 2300 was achieved. Unfortunately, theinfluence and popularity of these forecasters caused many technical traders to abandon their rules on Friday,October 16. The disaster that followed was a sober reminder that forecasters influence the market in differentways.

Markets were making a statement. As early as October 9, the Dow fell below 2450. This was considered a "critical"support.
There had been substantial "accumulation" beginning at 2400since late June. Investors who participated duringthe accumulation were subject to margin calls and selling panic on a dip below 2450. Yet, analysts refused to give uptheir optimism. Traders would not acknowledge that markets had run outof money.

It is surprising so many experts failed to realize 2300 was too far for the Dow to sustain. The late Augustcorrection resulted in a small but noticeable drop in S & P contract open interest. When the market rallied in early October, most of the accumulation was coming from the short hedging.

ThePsychologyoftheMarket

It is important that we understand how the human mind acts in its relation to market movements and affairs marketwise. The composite mind acts pretty much as the individual mind, but a mind below the average. That is why we have extremely unintelligent mass action.

The human mind has much interest in mystery, and operates largely on emotion and on catch words. Hope and fear are very large factors--especially unreasoned hope and fear, manipulators attempt to play on the moods of the outsiders by hints or some secret action relating to a stock, as that a "melon" is about to be out, that valuable "rights to subscribe to new stock area bout to be offered, that dividends are to be cut off, or government prosecution started, etc. It is excellent advice to painstakingly avoid being affected by any public attitude regarding the market of even Wall Street's attitude. Wall street is no exception to the rule of thecrowd psychology.

The human mind is more interested in the unknown than in the known. Whenthe unknown becomes the known, anticipated pleasure decreases and fear diminishes or vanishes.

Instincts such as greed are powerful market factors; they explain the "lambs" who try to make a fortune in a few turns of the wheel, as well as the ruthless menof large capital who operate a bear raid or a corner, using every trickthey know. Greed is a bad incentive for the stock market, and the "hog" is not popular in Wall Street, even when hemakes millions. Greed provides the incentive for many fatal rushes at the stock market in a bull market by the public, which buys at the top andlater pays. The man with the cooler head, whose brains master his cupidity, buys when stocks are cheap--even when there's a panic or depression.

The public sometimes comes into the market at the top, smelling "big profits," even when the advice to stay out is freely given. Thus, greed at the peak of a bull market and fear at the bottom of a bear market alike keep the instinct-ridden public from profiting. The more warnings given the public, the greater its lust, is a fact often to be observed.

It is obvious, then, that the time to beware is when there is a peak of optimism, and the time to open your purse is when everybody is imbuedwith pessimism. "The public always pays the freight" is thus seen to be axiomatic truth implicit in human nature.

Helpful Guidelines

Short selling is normally unsatisfactory because of the many risks involved. Nevertheless, a primary bear market does exists, perhaps such risk may not be out of bounds. Stock prices are far more likely to declinethan advance. Furthermore, itis possible that investors can substantially improve their risk-to-reward ratio by following some guidelines.

     1.   Don't buck the primary trend. Many inexperienced investors are tempted to short those stocks that have just skyrocketed on the assumption that suchstocks must be overpriced. But frequently, sudden market strength is followed by announcements of sharply increased earnings and dividends or other unexpected development that increase the underlying value of the stock. Moreover, many investors including major institutions, have a tendency to invest their capital in on the few issues that are in the limelight. Until such buyers have exhausted their resources, overpriced stocks often become more and more overpriced.

     2.   **Don't short thin issues.** Stocks with small floating supplies tend tofluctuate erratically. These issues could indeed tumble steeply in abear market. If manipulators decide to pool their resources and buy up the floating supply, short sellers could find themselves unable to repurchase the borrowed stocks without paying fabulous prices.

     3.   **Don't short stocks with large assets**. As the bear market progresses, many stocks will sell at substantial discounts from their asset values. Companies rich in liquidassets could become take over candidates. A surprise merger offer or liquidation announcement could cause these issues to jump sharply.

     4.   **Don'tshortstockspayinglargedividends.** Unless there are sound reasons to expect an imminent dividend cut,stocks with very large payouts shouldbe avoided. A safe andgenerous yield often provides a floor for the stock, especially since investors typically switch emphasis from growth to income in a bear market. For screening purposes, check the Relative Yield Index, which relates the stock's yield to prevailing conditions in the money market. Avoid those issues having an Index of over90.

     5.   **Don't get impatient.** Like buying stock long, short selling can be designed to trade against near-term fluctuations or capitalize onlonger-term trends. We don'tthink anyone should try to catch the short-term cycles--either on the long or short side. It involves costly commissions and is nerve-wracking as well.

Capitalizing on long-term terms, on the other hand, entails much less risk; changes in these trends can usually be anticipated with good accuracy. But such trends unfold slowly. The short-selling investor must therefore be prepared to hold the position for up to two or three years, if necessary.

6.   **Don't over-extend yourself.** To be flexible, you should vary the portion of your portfolio allocated to outright short sales. Try to practice the theory of contrary opinion by shorting more heavily when the mass is confident, reducing your shorts when the mass is turning worried, and covering your positions altogether when the mass is panicking. But at any rate, do not apply more than 50 percent of your portfolio to selling short. This will protect you from margin calls if your shorts run against you temporarily.

Short has-been glamours. On their way up, glamour issues with high price-earnings ratios should be avoided. But once these stocks top out they become avoided. But once these stocks top out they become highly suitable short candidates. This is especially true to companies that have passed their earnings growth peak. It is not necessary for earnings comparisons actually to turn unfavorable. For overpriced shares, the mere fact that the earnings growth rate is visibly slowing is usually sufficient to cause sharp declines.

7.   **Monitor institutional transactions.** In recent years, funds managed by the big banks have been one of the most disruptive forces in the stock market. Impatient buying or dumping has resulted in violent price movements. It is possible to make use of this force by shorting those stocks which are heavily held by such funds and which are beginning to be unloaded by them. Though a couple of months or so behind the fact, such information is regularly published by such financial magazines as "Barron's".

8.   **Update your evaluation.** Any investment position, whether long or short, must be continually reviewed. In the case of short selling, it is all the more important for you to ascertain at all times that the reasoning behind the original action is still valid. If things go wrong, take losses, if necessary, and use the capital elsewhere. Never, never be stubborn.

9.   Have courage of your convictions. Conversely, if you are reasonably sure that your analysis is meritable, don't let temporary reverses upset your judgment. Remember, for short periods of time the market can be quite irrational. The stocks you've shorted for the right reason could go up against you from time to time. But as long as primary bear market is under way, that stock will eventually succumb to free-market forces.

Best of Luck!